Inves Appraisal

Ken Langdon

- Fast track route to mastering the skills needed for evaluating return on investment

- Covers the key areas of return on investment, from cost benefit analysis and risk analysis to accounting techniques and the balanced scorecard

- Examples and lessons from some of the world's most successful businesses, including oil and telecommunications giants, and ideas from the smartest thinkers, including Mack Hanan and Warren Buffet

- Includes a glossary of key concepts and a comprehensive resources guide

≫EXPRESS EXEC.COM≪
essential management thinking at your fingertips

Copyright © Capstone Publishing 2002

The right of Ken Langdon to be identified as the author of this work has been asserted in accordance with the Copyright, Designs and Patents Act 1988

First published 2002 by
Capstone Publishing (a Wiley company)
8 Newtec Place
Magdalen Road
Oxford OX4 1RE
United Kingdom
http://www.capstoneideas.com

CIP catalogue records for this book are available from the British Library and the US Library of Congress

ISBN 1-84112-253-X

This book is printed on acid-free paper

Substantial discounts on bulk quantities of Capstone books are available to corporations, professional associations and other organizations. Please contact Capstone for more details on +44 (0)1865 798 623 or (fax) +44 (0)1865 240 941 or (e-mail) info@wiley-capstone.co.uk

Contents

Introduction to ExpressExec

ExpressExec is 3 million words of the latest management thinking compiled into 10 modules. Each module contains 10 individual titles forming a comprehensive resource of current business practice written by leading practitioners in their field. From brand management to balanced scorecard, ExpressExec enables you to grasp the key concepts behind each subject and implement the theory immediately. Each of the 100 titles is available in print and electronic formats.

Through the ExpressExec.com Website you will discover that you can access the complete resource in a number of ways:

» printed books or e-books;
» e-content – PDF or XML (for licensed syndication) adding value to an intranet or Internet site;
» a corporate e-learning/knowledge management solution providing a cost-effective platform for developing skills and sharing knowledge within an organization;
» bespoke delivery – tailored solutions to solve your need.

Why not visit www.expressexec.com and register for free key management briefings, a monthly newsletter and interactive skills checklists. Share your ideas about ExpressExec and your thoughts about business today.

Please contact elound@wiley-capstone.co.uk for more information.

Introduction

Who needs to know about return on investment?

» Uses for the Board
» Uses for middle managers
» Uses for private investors

"I will return. And I will be millions."
Inscription on the tomb of Eva Peron, Buenos Aires

If business projects could speak, Eva Peron's epitaph would be music to the businessperson's ears.

The essence of the role of a Board of Directors is to give shareholders an agreed return on the capital they are using in the business over an agreed period of time. This starts from the initial business plan where the founders of the company explain what products and services they will sell to which markets and in what volumes and values. They present this to their bankers or venture capitalists or friends and family if they are the source of the funds they need.

It continues when they go back for further finance; almost all projects funded by venture capital need at least one more round of financing before they become successful. The second time round probably causes more problems for the people running the business since their track record has changed from "unknown" to "hasn't made it yet."

On each occasion the providers of the capital are, in fact, asking a question that is impossible to answer. There are so many unknowns, particularly if both the product and the markets are new or innovative, that pinning down the business plan is like nailing a jelly to a wall.

And yet, it has to be done. Yes, there will be horrible inaccuracies. Yes, some of the racing certainties in the plan will come to nothing; but still someone needs to go through the process of estimating the income stream and costs of the new enterprise. The benefits of doing this are:

» it does give a rough idea of the financial consequences of the strategy;
» it makes certain that the managers have thought the project through;
» the managers can make their best estimates and then weigh them for risk;
» it gives the basis for a "contract," albeit a loose one between the funders and the funded;
» it allows people with different experience to give feedback to the managers, both their gut feel on the strategy and the lessons they have learnt; and

» it ensures that the flair and inventiveness of the people with the new idea has been exposed to the realities of business, and that they have understood enough of them to stand the questions of the funders

If this is true for a Board of Directors, who else benefits from having the skills involved in going through an exercise in return on investment? First of all - middle managers, the people delegated by the Board to deliver part of the overall plan. Sensible Boards of Directors require such people to put up business cases whenever they are applying for further resources for any sort of speculative activity - a new market, more people in the sales teams, or the purchase of some capital equipment to improve productivity in some way. Successful managers are those that are not fazed by a request for a business case, no matter how difficult this appears to begin with. How, for example, do you measure return on investment in a training program? Well, with some difficulty, but if a manager cannot connect expenditure on training with his or her objectives, why are they undertaking the training in the first place?

Getting good at making business cases will tend to separate one manager from another, to the benefit of the career of the person who takes the task on and does it well.

The second group of people who should take return on investment seriously are private investors. The ups and downs of the stock market make it difficult to know how your investments are progressing. If you cannot measure how they are progressing, then how do you know if they are going to achieve your objective in making the investment in the first place? Whether it was to build a pension fund or save for a child's education, you need to be able to plot the way. Looked at another way, if we laymen buy professionally run funds such as unit trusts and mutual finds, and are unable to work out how good an investment has been for us, then we deserve everything we get from the city slickers in the know who run those investments.

Return on investment is based on logic, but goes a long way beyond logic into emotion, gut feel, internal politics, economic stargazing, and so on. This book does not duck the issues that return on investment is a difficult combination of art and science, but it does maintain that everyone can do it, and that everyone should do it in a step-by-step logical fashion, with the occasional leap of faith and imagination.

Definition of Terms: What is Return on Investment?

Describes the logical steps involved in evaluating different investment opportunities.

» Covers the art of investment appraisal as practiced by managers predicting the future.
» Moves into the financial documentation you need to calculate RoI.

"Who controls the past controls the future; who controls the present controls the past."

George Orwell, 1984

Forgive me for a certain cynicism here; but that quote from Orwell is very apposite to the business world, when you consider return on investment. Managers are very different when they are estimating benefits that they will have to achieve if their leaders accept their proposition, than they are when demonstrating how successful a decision they took in the past has been.

Let's take an example. A sales manager, Sally, is discussing with one of her account managers the possibility of his taking on another salesperson. The account manager is keen to get the extra resource, since he knows that there is more business in his account if he can cover the ground more effectively. Sally is happy to find the money for the new person, but has to be convinced that she is putting her scarce resources into the most productive area. So, the answer to the first question "Will you sell more if we put another salesperson on your patch?" is easy: "Sure we will." The second question is much more difficult: "How much more?" Now consider what is going through the account manager's mind. He knows that if he claims a very high figure, say $5 mn, Sally may be skeptical but will be sufficiently impressed probably to let him have the resource. But at what cost? She will, of course, change the estimate into a management objective, and the account manager's target will go up by $5 mn or an amount which recognizes that it will take a while to get the new person up to speed. If, on the other hand, the account manager goes low, saying "Well for the first year I think we must allow a settling in period and maybe expect $100,000," there are probably other sales managers who will offer Sally a better deal than this and she will prefer to give them the resource. So he has to go somewhere between these two. He wants to be successful and to be seen to be successful. This means that he would rather take a target of $900,000 and make $950,000 than take a target of $1 mn and get $950,000. The first is success; the second is failure. And so his thoughts go on. He will try to agree a number that he really believes he can achieve, but will be attractive enough to get Sally's agreement to the hiring of the person.

This may seem to lack some logic, but actually if everyone is competent at their jobs it can work quite well. An experienced account manager will probably be able to give a reasonable estimate of what his or her resources will bring in. It is, after all, one of the things they are there for.

This example is typical of the way parameters for investment appraisal are set and how decisions are discussed and arrived at, particularly in big companies. Middle managers are encouraged to have ideas, to estimate the benefits of the idea, and convince their managers that they should be allowed to go ahead. Most are circumspect and cautious about their claims, but some do have a rush of blood to the head and claim huge, but unbelievable, results for their pet project. To deal with both the optimist and the pessimist, organizations need a process that examines ideas dispassionately. This is called the Investment Appraisal system, and includes the calculation of Return on Investment. Put very simply, Return on Investment, (RoI) is a method of comparing the use of a company's or an individual's cash for one investment project with another. It is also a perfectly good way of testing projects that have been implemented to see whether they have achieved the results that management told their bosses or their shareholders they were aiming at.

Let's examine the use of historical return on investment, sometimes rather rudely referred to as "post-hoc cost justification" a little further. Suppose that Sally, the sales manager, had two years ago bought a computer system aimed at capturing and making available to the salesforce prospecting information with contact names and addresses, and space to describe when the last contact was made, and what the current situation is. Sally will, two years ago, have had to bear the interrogation of her boss as to what the return on investment would be. She would have ducked and dived a bit, because saying that it would improve sales results would be hard to prove, and even harder to quantify. In whatever way she persuaded the boss to part with the money, she will deal very differently if asked, say by the IT department looking to check the benefits of the systems they provide, what good the system has done over the two years. She will almost certainly find the best possible interpretation of her results to show that the decision she made was an excellent one that has succeeded in reaching all the objectives set for it, particularly the financial ones. The psychology has changed, with the manager eagerly ascribing benefits to their decision, as opposed, in the predicting the future RoI, to building a rod for her own back.

INTRODUCTION TO RETURN ON INVESTMENT

It is an interesting fact that when you are a manager you find that whenever a member of your team asks to see you, as opposed to you asking to see them, they are almost certainly going to ask for resources. It is the manager's job to look at all the possibilities and decide which will give them the best return on investment in the short and long term. In conjunction with a business case template, the subject of Chapter 6, managers need to put the options through an investment appraisal process.

The following steps define the process of evaluation:

» choose a timescale;
» estimate the benefits;
» estimate the costs;
» weigh up the risks to the costs and benefits;
» produce a projected profit and loss account;
» produce a cashflow;
» compare possible projects, along with their risks, with each other and with a benchmark.

We will take these one at a time as we examine how companies decide how to invest their resources.

CHOOSE A TIMESCALE

Most investment opportunities need in the first place a combination of capital expenditure, which is mainly on fixed assets, and revenue expenditure, money to finance the people and other running costs. Fixed assets have a depreciation period agreed by the finance people to be a reasonable estimate of the productive life of the asset. This depreciation period is frequently the timescale chosen to measure the viability of a project involving capital expenditure.

Some finance departments set a number of company norms for the timescale of justifying fixed assets. They may believe that three years is the maximum amount of time that a vehicle will be useful to the company. Plant and machinery is given a much longer life of five to ten years, depending on the speed with which the technologies being purchased are changing. It will be shorter where there is a large element of software involved in the purchase. Computer equipment is difficult. Everyone who is involved in buying this technology knows that something two keystrokes better will be available in the very near future even when you have just made an investment, so some accountants take a three-year view on computers to be used internally but demand that equipment to be used in providing a service to customers must justify itself within 18 months.

Another element in the decision on timescales is the length of time it takes for the project to get started. It would be less than useful to measure the benefit of building, for example, a tunnel between England and France without taking into account that from inception to operation the project will take more than 10 years. For the finances to work in such a project its revenue earning life will need to be extended to perhaps 50 years.

In the end, timescales for investment appraisal should be sensible. They should reflect the real life of the project, and if it is known at the start that further investment will be required during the time chosen, then that expenditure should be added into the equation.

Currently the mood of finance people and chief executives is to take into account how volatile and changeable the business world is becoming, and to reduce the timescale a project has to succeed. This defends them from agreeing to projects that become unviable before profitability is reached. The ExpressExec software tool, Return on Investment, uses three years as its norm for that reason.

ESTIMATE THE BENEFITS

This is perhaps the most difficult part of the estimating process. As we have seen, it often has an emotional overtone with managers who are making the estimates while aware that they will turn into increased targets or stiffer objectives if the expenditure is approved. It is useful for estimating reasons, and also for risk analysis, as we will see, to break the benefits into three categories:

» reduction in costs;
» avoidance of future costs; and
» revenue growth,

Let's take these one at a time.

Reduction in costs

In assessing a spending project this area is likely to be very important. Finance people are likely to agree that a reduction of costs is the most tangible benefit there is. You have to make sure that the costs claimed as a reduction are *relevant costs*. For example, a Telecommunications Manager is trying to cost justify the purchase of a new telephone switchboard for his company. He knows that the new switch has a smaller "footprint" than the old one. The old one took up some 225 square meters, while the new switch will only take up half of that. The accommodation where it sits is very expensive at £300 per square meter. He wants to claim a saving of half of the cost of the accommodation – an impressive £33,750 per annum. But unfortunately this is an unavoidable cost and irrelevant to this telephone replacement project. Unless he can sublet surplus space, unlikely in this circumstance, or unless the lease was coming up for renewal and he can go elsewhere, he will not be allowed to claim this as a reduction in cost.

Most importantly, the manager who will have to take a drop in expenditure budget, since that is how the cost reduction will be realized, must agree any reduction in cost. As we saw with increases in sales, many managers also respond very cautiously to an argument that they can do with less budget. In the end, business cases are well made when reductions in costs outweigh the expenses of the project. Other benefits will make a reasonable case into a good one. Remember that estimates are not facts; they are negotiable. The agreement of a manager to a small percentage saving in a large cost can have a dramatic effect on the business case.

Avoidance of future costs

The avoidance of future costs is a slightly different concept to a straightforward reduction in costs. This brings into the business case for a project costs which would be incurred if the project were not undertaken. This is often illustrated by a decision between contracting or expanding a poorly performing business. Do you down size it to a point where it makes a profit or you are out of the business, or do you expand it so that it gets into a position to give a satisfactory return? In building a business case for expansion a manger can make the point that expansion will avoid the cost of paying off excess staff. Once again, the test is to make sure that the cost to be avoided is real.

Increases in revenue

The top line of any proposed profit and loss account is sales. This is true whether the sales are external, to the company's customers, or internal, to other departments within the business. Expenditure of money will often have as the first part of the justification claims that revenues will increase.

Most times when estimating revenues you will need to use a range of results. The most common method of doing this is to take three possibilities:

» worst case – the lowest outcome which you believe possible;
» expected case – your view of what will actually happen; and
» best case – the best, but still feasible, outcome.

This adds to the reliability of the business case and is helpful in deciding on the amount of risk there is in the project.

Any project that purports to improve management control will more than likely have to prove its worth through offering revenue growth. Companies are continuously re-engineering their business processes. If they change their strategy in any way or react to changes in technology, they will almost certainly have to review some of their business processes. This almost always ends up with capital and revenue expenditure and is often justified by the fact that it affords management better control over the business. This may be good enough for the people running the business, but it is not sufficiently concrete for the finance department. They want to know how this benefit will turn into cash.

Improvements in control can be difficult to quantify as revenue growth, but, if you do not, the finance people will not let you put them in the business case.

ESTIMATE THE COSTS

In comparison with benefits, costs are more straightforward to estimate. You will find they fall into the categories of staff, equipment rental, depreciation of purchased assets, facilities, and consumables. It is always better to agree costs with a supplier, since this passes the risk that they might be wrong onto them rather than you. Once again, make sure that the costs are relevant. Here is an example.

The accommodation benefit in the telephone switchboard example above is matched in this case by the irrelevance of a cost that might be thought to come into this project equation. Consider a project where a company is considering the installation of a new IT facility. This would be housed in one of the offices currently occupied by administration. Of the three people currently occupying that office, one is due for retirement and will not be replaced, and the others can be found a home elsewhere in the administration offices.

Many would suggest that the proposed IT facility should suffer its share of total company rent based on the floor area of the office. This does not make sense. The company is paying exactly the same amount of rent, whether it adopts this new project or not. There are no new costs of rent and therefore rent is irrelevant to this decision.

It may well be that the internal management P&L account will show part of the rent apportioned to the IT department, but this does not make it relevant to the investment decision.

In investment appraisal you need to look very carefully at fixed and variable costs to make sure that you do not load irrelevant costs onto the project being analyzed. The test is whether the costs react to changes in activity level.

In a bookshop, for example, the cost of books sold will vary almost exactly in proportion to sales whereas salaries, rates, repairs etc. will change only by steps. These fixed costs are constant in total throughout a particular range of sales. For example, it would be possible to sell a lot more books before it became necessary to take on extra staff.

In project appraisal, you should not apportion a share of existing fixed costs against new projects. On the other hand, if a new project causes an increase in fixed costs, then the whole of that increase is a relevant cost of the project.

WEIGH UP THE RISKS TO THE COSTS AND BENEFITS

We have said that no estimate for the future will be exact; there will always be the unexpected as well as the normal tolerance to be expected in a prediction. Before you move to the step of producing the estimated profit and loss account, take time out to look at the risks in the benefits and costs. Risks to the benefits are that fewer than your prediction will occur, or that they will not occur in the timescale predicted. Risks to the costs are that they will be greater than budget, either because your estimate is wrong, or because delay has cost money. There are a number of occasions in the return on investment process when different forms of risk analysis are useful. Here is one used at an early stage in the process.

We have already seen one of the ways of taking risk into account, which is to produce a range of forecasts; pessimistic, most likely, and optimistic. Let's take that technique a step further.

Remember the types of benefit we identified. Another example of a risk matrix using the benefit type as the grouping is given in Table 2.1.

Table 2.1

	Worst case	Expected case	Best case
Reduce costs	1	3	6
Avoid costs	2	5	8
Revenue growth	4	7	9

Experience allows us to give each cell in the matrix a number from 1 to 9 in the order of confidence that we should have that the benefit will be achieved. It goes from the most likely to occur, the worst case estimate for a cost reduction, to the least likely, a best case estimate for a benefit in revenue growth.

Assuming we know the costs involved in the project, we can now calculate whether this is a high- or low-risk project. Add up all the benefits from the cells marked 1–3. If that produces a number which is greater than the costs, then the project can be termed low risk. If you have to go down to 8 or 9 before the costs are covered, you have a project that carries a high risk that the project will not be profitable.

Don't forget that the objective of risk analysis is not only to identify what the risks are, but also to do something about them. If, for example, there was some doubt about the benefits in cell 5, and that doubt was the difference between a medium- and high-risk project, you might be inclined to do some more investigation to improve the estimate, or resolve to put extra resources into making sure that during the implementation of the project the benefits in that cell are actually realized.

The simplest way of ameliorating the risk of underbudgeting is to put contingency money into both the start-up costs of a project and the continuing revenue spend. Many companies build contingency into their investment appraisal technique as a norm. So you have to put into the profit and loss account an extra 10% capital spend for contingency, and an extra 10% contingency on the running costs.

PRODUCE A PROJECTED PROFIT AND LOSS ACCOUNT

A project profit and loss account looks like any other profit and loss account except in the level of detail. Whereas a profit and loss account in management or financial accounting might have only three descriptions of costs, cost of sales, selling and distribution costs, and administrative overheads, a project profit and loss account will have the detail of these.

PRODUCE A CASHFLOW

It is quite possible for a company to be making profits but failing for lack of cash. One of the main reasons for this is that the profit and loss account will show the cost of fixed assets being spread over a period of time by depreciation, whereas when a company buys a fixed asset the cash has to be paid out immediately. For this reason companies will always look at cashflow forecasts as well as the projected profit and loss account when considering the future.

Similarly, when we appraise an individual project we need to consider the effect on both cash and profit.

A very important point in return on investment calculation is that we are trying to consider the effect of a new project on a company. Establishing how the company would perform without the new project and comparing this with how it would perform with the new project will assist managers to make the correct decision. It may, however, not be accurate to compare performance before and after the introduction of the project, since changes may be due to other factors.

This brings us to a more general question as to which cashflows are relevant when evaluating a new project. The general principle is that a cashflow is only relevant in evaluating a project if it changes as a result of the introduction of that project. We have already seen some of the effects of this in terms of making sure that you are dealing with relevant costs and benefits.

How we do it

Essentially, converting a budgeted P&L account into a cashflow forecast is a matter of considering the timing of payments.

If we are preparing monthly budgets and cashflow then there will be a lot of differences as shown in Table 2.2.

When, however, we look at longer term projects we do not often attempt to budget on a monthly, or even quarterly, basis. It is more usual to produce annual cashflows. In this case, most of the differences between cashflow and profit are ignored with the exception of depreciation.

KEY LEARNING POINTS

Let's try to summarize the answer to the title of this chapter in a few words. A key role of management is to examine future plans

Table 2.2

Item	Profit and loss account	Cashflow
Sales revenue	Include when sold	Include when cash is collected
Cost of sales	Match with sales	Not applicable
Purchases	Not applicable	Allow for the purchase to be made some time before the sale, but recognize that payment is made some time after purchase
Depreciation	According to policy	Not applicable
Fixed assets	Not applicable	Include when paid for
Other expenses and interest	Include on accruals basis, that is, when incurred	Include when paid

as a series of projects that they can evaluate by using techniques of return on investment. The techniques themselves form a logical set of steps:

1 estimate what will happen in terms of costs and benefits; and
2 weight the costs and benefits for risk.

This is the art of return on investment, as managers try to become accurate at predicting the future.

The rest of the process:

3 turns these predictions into a profit and loss account; and
4 produces a cashflow.

From these we can move in later chapters to a consistent and relevant comparison of one investment project with another.

Evolution of Return on Investment

Managers have progressed from a simple "when do I break even?" question, into more advanced techniques that eliminate the inconsistencies caused by the timing of project costs and income.

» Payback method of RoI and Average return on capital employed
» Discounted cashflows and the internal rate of return

"Forecasts can be injurious to your wealth."
Dean LeBaron, b.1933, investment manager

The final step of investment appraisal is the financial calculation and comparison. The notion of return on investment has, like other business techniques, evolved over time. Simple early techniques suited managers looking for a quick method of making sure they were not making a mistake, but dropped short of what the financial people would describe as logically viable. The techniques used become more sophisticated as projects become bigger and carry bigger risks.

Compare possible projects, along with their risks, with each other and with a benchmark.

Before coming to the main method used by most business people to calculate return on investment, discounted cashflow, it is useful to look at what went before. The inadequacies of simpler to calculate formulae pushed finance people into a more sophisticated approach. But to begin with, most business people become easily familiar with the payback period method of calculating return on investment.

PAYBACK PERIOD

This method measures the length of time from the first payment of cash until the total receipts of cash from the investment equals the total payment made on that investment. In other words, "How long does it take to get my money back?" It does not in any way attempt to measure the profitability of projects and restricts all calculations to a receipts and payments basis.

In considering alternative projects, managers using the payback method obviously prefer the project with the shortest payback period. Here is a comparison of two projects using payback period (Table 3.1).

In this case the second project would be preferred despite the fact that the positive cashflow for project 1 ramps up in the fifth year.

The payback method has the advantage of being quick and simple, but it has two major disadvantages as well.

» It considers only cash received during the payback period and ignores anything received afterwards.
» It does not take into account the dates on which the cash is actually received. So, it is possible to have two projects both costing the

Table 3.1

	Project 1	Project 2
Cost of purchasing the assets	£10,000	£15,000
Net cashflow		
Year 1	2,000	3,000
Year 2	3,000	4,000
Year 3	3,000	6,000
Year 4	4,000	8,000
Year 5	10,000	2,000
Payback period	3.5 years	3.25 years

Table 3.2

	Project1	Project2
Asset cost	£10,000	£10,000
Net cashflow		
Year 1	1,000	3,000
Year 2	3,000	3,000
Year 3	3,000	3,000
Year 4	3,000	1,000
Year 5	4,000	4,000
Payback period	4 years	4 years

same, with the same payback period, but with different cashflows, such that one has a better, earlier cashflow than the other.

In the next example the two projects have the same payback period. However, it is obvious that, without any further information, we should prefer project two since the cash is received earlier, and can therefore be reinvested in another project to earn more profits (Table 3.2).

It is in fact very difficult to know which of these projects is better for the business simply by using the payback method of investment appraisal.

The payback method has some disadvantages, but is still in use for quite complex projects. This is particularly true where there is a great deal of early capital investment in infrastructure followed by a lengthy period of income derived from those assets. A telephone operator is a good example of such a company. They have to lay down the telephone network before they can start to earn revenues with it – a massive cash investment.

Here is an actual example, renamed to protect commercial confidentiality. The PTV Cable Television Company, a cable operator, was planning its move into telephony. It was already a successful operator of its television franchise and had a predicted cashflow as shown in Table 3.3.

When do the annual cashflows of this enterprise go positive? Simply check along the Cashflow (000's) line and see that year 6 is positive. When does the project break even? You get this from the next line, the net cashflow to date, or cumulated cashflow. It breaks even during year 10. This is a very useful number, since you can ask a number of "what if?" questions and see what that does to break-even. In fact, we can test the telephony project by looking at its impact on break-even (Table 3.4).

The answers to the same questions asked about television are that the annual cashflows also go positive in Year 6 when you add in telephony, and the break-even date for telephony happens in Year 8.

Suppose the business case template for the company included the criteria "Any new project in addition to television must not delay the time that the company has a positive cashflow, and must not delay when the project reaches break-even." In both cases this project conforms.

This method of calculating return on investment also allows us to answer some other crucial questions. How much money will the company have to have available to fund the television project? Look for the largest number on the net cashflow line and you find the answer is 149,302,000. How much additionally will it need to go into telephony? The number is 21,005,991 for the same reason.

Getting such a lot of large figures down to just two or three crucial ones shows the payback method of investment appraisal being very useful in decision-making.

Return on Capital Employed (ROCE)

It can be argued that an improved version of payback is arrived at if you average out the benefits stream over the life of the project. That is what the return on capital employed does (Table 3.5).

Table 3.3 PTV Television cashflow.

	Year 1	Year 2	Year 3	Year 4	Year 5	Year 6	Year 7	Year 8	Year 9	Year 10
Cashflow (000s)	−55,610	−25,283	−27,308	−25,635	−15,466	22,056	34,060	42,716	50,249	58,919
Net cashflow to date	−55,610	−80,893	−108,201	−133,836	−149,302	−127,246	−93,186	−50,470	−221	58,698

Table 3.4 PTV Telephony cashflow.

	Year 1	Year 2	Year 3	Year 4	Year 5	Year 6	Year 7	Year 8	Year 9	Year 10
Total revenue	0	2,312,430	9,078,105	18,208,411	28,959,467	36,607,290	39,151,025	41,453,356	43,891,662	46,474,006
Interconnect charges	0	1,331,776	5,237,458	10,565,948	16,917,647	21,457,301	22,985,321	24,375,933	25,850,676	27,414,642
Billing costs	0	188,370	733,466	1,422,455	2,170,951	2,689,880	2,852,903	2,995,548	3,145,325	3,302,592
Administration cost	0	1,077,492	1,929,373	3,067,009	4,401,236	5,365,280	5,719,148	6,046,479	6,392,680	6,758,845
Total costs	0	2,597,638	7,900,297	15,055,413	23,489,834	29,512,460	31,557,372	33,417,960	35,388,682	37,476,079
Operating cashflow	0	−285,207	1,177,808	3,152,999	5,469,633	7,094,830	7,593,653	8,035,396	8,502,981	8,997,927
Capital expenditure	0	9,008,514	7,190,271	6,422,786	7,899,653	583,097	0	0	0	0
Cashflow	0	−9,293,721	−6,012,463	−3,269,787	−2,430,020	6,511,733	7,593,653	8,035,396	8,502,981	8,997,927
Net cashflow to date	0	−9,293,721	−15,306,184	−18,575,972	−21,005,991	−14,494,259	−6,900,606	1,134,790	9,637,771	18,635,698

Table 3.5

Asset cost	£10,000
Estimated residual value	NIL
Expected earnings (before depreciation)	
Year 1	2,000
Year 2	3,000
Year 3	5,000
Year 4	7,000
Year 5	8,000
Total	£25,000
Net earnings over 5 years	£15,000
Average earnings	£3,000
Average Return on Capital Employed	30% (3,000/10,000)

It is sometimes argued that the average capital employed of £5,000 should be used instead of £10,000. On this basis, the answer to the previous example would be 60%. Either method can be employed as long as this is done consistently.

Once again, however, return on capital employed has the disadvantage that it does not take into account the time when the return is received. Thus it is possible to have two projects having the same ROCE, yet for one project to start immediately, and for the other to have a pre-production period of, say, two years.

Discounted cashflow

We are agreed then, that we need a method of investment appraisal that takes into account the timing of the cashflows as well as their absolute amount. Discounted cashflow (DCF) does just that. Look at it this way.

Suppose I offer to give you $1000. Would you prefer to have it now or in five years' time? Obviously now, since if you want to spend the money it will be worth more now than it will be after five years of even modest inflation. But what if you don't need to spend it now? Then you still want the use of it so that you could put it somewhere it will earn money, sometimes called the opportunity cost of money. You will therefore have more to spend in five years' time.

But you have assumed that I am paying no interest in the five years. Suppose I say that if you take it in five years' time I will pay you 50% per annum interest. Now, of course, you would prefer to wait. In five years' time I will give you $7,593.75. Even if you needed to spend the money now, you could borrow it, pay interest, and still have a hefty profit in five years.

The concept of discounted cashflow is based on the usefulness of being able to calculate what interest percentage I would have to pay you for it to make no difference at all whether you take the money now or in five years. We know it is somewhere between 0 and 50%.

The mechanics of discounted cashflow

To arrive at a method of doing this, consider the following.

You have inherited £10,000 from Aunt Mary. Unfortunately, she had heard that you are liable to spend money fairly freely so the will says that you cannot receive the cash until your thirtieth birthday. You are 27 today (Happy Birthday!).

Aunt Mary was actually fairly well informed. You are desperate to get this money before lunchtime tomorrow in order to place a bet on a horse someone has told you is going to do well in the 2.30 race. You have found a friendly banker who will advance you part of the money.

The interest rate is 10% per annum and she is prepared to advance you an amount A, such that with interest you will owe the bank exactly £10,000 in three years' time. How much can you get?

If you borrow £100 now, you will owe interest of £10 by the end of one year so the total outstanding will be £110.

During the second year, interest will be charged on the total amount outstanding of £110, i.e. interest of £11. The total outstanding would be £121.

During the third year, interest will be charged on the total amount outstanding of £121, i.e. interest of £12.10. The total outstanding would then be £133.10.

We can see therefore that for every £100 borrowed, £133.10 must be repaid.

Therefore, solving the equation:

$$A \times 1.331 = £10,000$$

will tell us how much can be borrowed now, i.e. about £7,510.

Table 3.6

Timing of cashflow	Amount of cashflow	Discount factor at 10%	Present Value
Immediate	(10,000)	1	(10,000)
After 1 year	3,000	0.909	2,727
After 2 years	4,000	0.826	3,304
After 3 years	5,000	0.751	3,755
After 4 years	3,000	0.683	2,049
Net present value			£1,835

This technique can of course be generalized to deal with any rate of interest and any time period.

We can now develop a method to compare two projects. Cashflows due in the future may be converted to equally desirable cashflows due today using the above method. This technique is know as discounting and the equivalent cashflow due today is known as a present value (Table 3.6).

Discount factors may be found from tables or by using the formula:

$1/(1 + i)n$

where i = discount rate and n = number of years.

In particular, consider the discount factor used above for year 3, i.e. 0.751. When deciding how much we could borrow from the bank in respect of Aunt Mary's bequest we divided £10,000 by 1.331. It is an exactly equivalent calculation to multiply £10,000 by 0.751 – the discount factor for three years at 10%.

The final result takes into account all cashflows by totaling them and is known as the net present value of the project.

If compelled to choose between two projects, we will select the one with the higher net present value. If we have a large number of projects, many of which can be undertaken, then we would wish to invest in every project with a positive net present value.

Comments on using discounted cashflows

1 The initial investment occurs at time 0, the start of the project. Further cashflows then arise throughout the first year but all of these

are combined to give one figure for the whole year. This one net cashflow is then treated as though it all arose on the first anniversary of the initial investment. Similarly, all of the cashflows during the second year are combined to give the year 2 cashflow and so on. If it is absolutely necessary to make the calculations more accurate, cashflows could be allocated to shorter periods (e.g. quarters) and the appropriate discount factors used.

2 However, most companies would not consider it worthwhile to use shorter periods because the extra accuracy achieved is hardly worthwhile, bearing in mind that all of the data is estimated. Further, combining all of the interim cashflows into one year usually results in a more cautious approach to project appraisal; that is, it tends to diminish the net present value.

3 Cashflows must be relevant costs and benefits as explained previously.

4 The discount rate represents the cost of capital. In a large company the Treasury Function will lay this down. Indeed, if you work for a large company and are involved in investment appraisal, make sure that you known what their discount factor is. It may be the same as its notional cost of capital or it may be much higher. Some companies want technology projects, for example, to give a positive NPV when tested against a discount factor of 15% or greater.

5 Projects with a positive net present value add to the value of the company and if they are OK against other business-case template criteria should generally be accepted.

6 There is another numerical concept called the internal rate of return or IRR. Remember the question "When would you like to be given $1,000?" We said then that it was possible to work out an interest rate that would make it completely immaterial whether you took the money now or later. This is the IRR, the discount factor at which the NPV is reduced to zero.

Would you rather have 10% of $50 million, or 20% of $5 million? An easy question, but if you make decisions based only on the IRR, you may well opt for the second. Always use the NPV for decision-making.

Here is another example of DCF at work. A company has a project under consideration, shown in Table 3.7.

Table 3.7

Timing of cashflow	Amount of cashflow at 15% value	Discount factor	Present
Immediate	(20,000)	1.00	(20,000)
After 1 year	10,000	0.870	8,700
After 2 years	8,000	0.756	6,048
After 3 years	6,000	0.658	3,948
Net present value			(1,304)

Since the net present value is negative, the company should reject this project if its business template requires projects to return 10% or more.

You may think that the above is so simplified that there is much more to learn before you can use the technique in practice. This is just not so. The difficulty is in establishing the cashflows that should go into the computation. Once this has been done, the mechanics do not change whether we are dealing with the Channel Tunnel or buying a simple machine.

The discounted cashflow is probably the most important technique used in investment appraisal. Once you have internalized it you are in a position to calculate return on investment for any business decision you have to make, and many personal ones as well. You can also use it to measure the return on investment of a portfolio of shares (see Chapter 6). You can use it in your personal life to calculate, for example, the best way to borrow money to buy a property. Indeed, if you think about personal finance advisers and others who sell us pensions and mutual funds, subjecting their suggestions to the rigors of a discounted cashflow would force them to be more open about what they are proposing.

KEY LEARNING POINTS

1 There are some simple methods of comparing the financial results of different investment opportunities.

2 The simpler techniques are vulnerable to error caused by the value of money at the time it changes hands.

3 The financial technique that gives the most accurate answer is the discounted cashflow.

4 The DCF technique makes it possible to compare two or more projects with costs and income happening at different times, by eliminating the time element by discounting it to a present-day value.

The E-Dimension

When investors were challenged with valuing companies in the new Internet environment they chucked out the old rules.

» How the market valued Internet companies that had not as yet traded
» How very major telecommunications companies made huge mistakes in investment appraisal

"Hysterical 'bulls' care nothing whatever about the earnings or dividend return on a stock. The only note to which they attune their actions is the optimistic slogan, 'It's going up!' and the higher it goes, the more they buy, and the more their ranks are swelled by new recruits."

Henry Howard Harper (1926) The Psychology of Speculation

If I had not put in the date that Harper wrote that quotation, you might easily have guessed that he was talking about the extraordinary performance of the shares of companies that purported to, or in some cases actually did, aim to make sales and profits by offering various products and services using the Internet during the latter half of the 1990s.

Lest I be accused of being very smart after the event, and one of the huge group of people who, after the crash of these shares, were heard to declare that they told you so, and that they had foreseen the end to the bubble, let me admit that both my self-administered pension fund and the investment club I belong to lost a good deal of money when the crash arrived. We both took some profits, so it was not a wipeout, but it put us back a good bit.

So, how did it happen? In the main you have to agree with Harper that it was an emotional, illogical phenomenon. People rushed to put money into companies that had never made any sales, let alone any profits. Venture capitalists and other professionals put huge sums of money into these companies, giving them stratospheric price/earnings ratios. The entrepreneurs, mainly young people with a passion and flair for things to do with the Internet, spent that money fairly recklessly in the hope of huge profits to come. The profits arose in a very small number of them, and the start-up money became dissipated. Probably the only people who got rich from the Internet boom were the original entrepreneurs, if they had the sense to cash in some of their chips at or near the top, and the venture capitalists who had good exit strategies before the great bookmaker in the sky called time.

We can perhaps draw one or two lessons in terms of return on investment by looking at how so many people's hopes of huge and quick returns turned to ashes. First of all we will look at how Internet companies were valued to justify the heady heights to which their shares rose. Next it might be useful to look at one case where – I am speculating here, not having any inside knowledge – the company's strategy became so crucial to an investment decision that it looked as though the other rules of good investment appraisal were ignored.

VALUING AN INTERNET COMPANY

How do you value an investment that is at the start of a major new way of doing things? A lot of people believe that what happened with Internet stocks was similar to what happened to car stocks a hundred years ago, and railway stocks even earlier, when they first started to trade. The opportunity was so huge, perhaps every adult in the country will eventually have an automobile, and the way ahead so unknown that it was necessary to chuck the old rules of valuing companies, boring things like profitability, liquidity, asset utilization, and productivity, in favor of a new paradigm. Here is how it was done for the Internet phenomenon.

The stock market appeared convinced that a large proportion of sales transactions were going to be carried out using the Internet in years to come. Many companies were, and still are, changing their selling environments to cater for this, and specialist companies started up with the sole purpose of exploiting this type of selling channel. But how do you value them, when growth is going to take 10 years to get to the potential?

"Easy," said the market, "Take the market size for the industry sector and project it out 10 years. If it is, for example, global transactions in food and drink, then it will be an incredibly high figure in the trillions of dollars. You get it by looking at how much food and drink is bought and sold throughout the world each year now and allowing for annual growth, as people eat more, there are more people eating, and they can afford more convenient, and therefore more expensive, food. Now look at a company that has started work on developing the systems and customer base to allow these transactions to occur on-line. Some of them have spent hundreds of millions of dollars to get ready. Allow that they, the market leaders of the future, will have a proportion of those transactions, say 10%, and you have another very high number. Assume that they can make a profit of 20% on these sales and allow that that represents their profit stream in 10 years' time, still a very large figure.

"You can then turn to the well-trusted technique of investment appraisal – discounted cashflow. Discount the profit figure back to present value. Use the discount rate of 2–3% above depositor interest rate to allow for risk. That present value now represents what the company would be earning now and can be used as the earnings side of the price/earnings (P/E) ratio. Give it a conservative P/E of 10, which means you multiply it by 10 to get the present value of the business." Since we started in trillions, we are still in billions by the time we get to this figure.

This explains how companies such as Amazon.com and eBay.com had market valuations in billions of dollars before they started to make a profit at all. Was the market right? Well, that is up to you. There is an argument for buying shares which are out of fashion rather than the subject of huge bull market pressure, but the late nineties' performance of Internet shares suggested the opposite. People filled their boots with shares that were showing growth of hundreds of percent per annum, in order not to miss out on the really high returns available on the stock market.

So it all came crashing down. Many shares joined the 90% club; an elite set of shares whose low was more than 90% less than their high. Perhaps the learning message from all of this is just the very old one, if a return on investment looks too good to be true, then it probably is too good to be true.

DRIVEN BY THE STRATEGY

Good managers, and more especially good directors, should have a healthy cynicism against cries from their colleagues that "There is no alternative, we simply have to do it, it is strategic to the whole future of the business." I have been using the following mantra for so long that I do not know who to credit with having said it first. "If you must have an answer today, the answer is no."

Despite the paucity of choice that Henry Ford famously made available to his customers – "You can have any color as long as it is black" – Ford trained his people in the opposite, and insisted that any decision that anyone was going to ask him to make had to have alternatives.

Consider then many of the biggest telephone network operators around Europe at the beginning of this century. Their strategies had been for many years globalization and subscriber-to-subscriber connection. This latter meant that they all wanted to have fixed and mobile networks and it seems to me that they could not conceive of an alternative to this.

Along comes the promise of third generation mobile phones. This required a new network infrastructure and offered considerably enhanced mobile capability to users. In order to be able to offer 3G, the network operators had to buy from their Governments the license to use the necessary bandwidth. It was expected that these would be expensive, but 3G returns were also expected to be very large, so the auction started.

One can imagine a company like BT in the UK producing its business case to justify the bids they were putting in to remain competitive in each round of bidding against their rivals. One can also imagine the finance people being pretty much rolled by the "We have just got to be on the third generation battle ground" into allowing more and more optimistic estimates of the 3G income stream to go into the return on investment calculations.

Eventually the deal was done, the companies paid much more than they could afford and they ran up such huge levels of debt that their credit ratings were reduced. Ironically, the way out of the debt mountain was to sell off parts of the business, the opposite of the initial strategy that had got them into trouble. The first moral of this story is much the same as the Internet companies boom and bust – don't let old and trusted techniques of management go hang because you find yourself in a new situation with an old strategy. Imagine if the board of BT had had the vision to drop out of the bidding at a late stage. They could probably have bought the license from one of the big bidders when they realized they did not have the cash to buy the license and build the network. But old strategies die hard.

There is a second return on investment moral from the same story. Technology projects are notoriously difficult to put a reliable timescale to. Most software projects, for example, go over time and over budget for this very reason. This is partly because it is genuinely difficult to predict how long it will take to produce a new piece of technology, and partly because the squeeze goes on the technology people from the marketing people who want it next year or it will be too late. The competition will have got in first. It is very hard to resist the marketing logic, and technologists strip out the time they have set aside as contingency in order to come up with a timescale that suits functional managers. This adds mightily to the risk of the project.

We can be pretty sure that this occurred on third generation technology as well, since shortly after the licenses were bought, it became obvious that the technology would be late, and that the business cases were based on income streams that were reckoned to start anything from 18 months to three years before the actuality.

KEY LEARNING POINT

If a project fails against the rules of financial evaluation, consider changing the project rather than changing the rules.

The Global Dimension

Risk and return are subject to cultural differences like any other facet of business. Building a global return on investment process needs to bear this in mind if it is to implement its risk and return strategy.

» Balancing central control with empowerment
» Looking at a strategy that gets it right
» Learning on a global basis

"Most companies have had the word 'globalization' built into their language for some time, but few have completely understood how much they have to empower the local people to make this happen."

Trevor Merriden (2001) Business the Nokia Way.
Capstone, Oxford

Globalization and return on investment raise a number of topics that are interlinked. Investors seeking a good return need to understand how well companies they are considering investing in are handling globalization. Companies need to find a good balance between central control, to ensure that branding and human resources management is consistent across the world, with the requirement to empower local management teams to enable them to make investment decisions that reflect their local needs. The third topic in this chapter concerns learning globally. It is now possible for companies to use their intranets and knowledge systems to make sure that an investment decision taken in one part of the world can be accessed and learnt from in any other location.

GLOBALIZATION AND RETURN ON INVESTMENT PROCESSES

The fashion for seeking global branding continues into this millennium, but it is now tempered by the realization that altering names, packaging, and advertising so that your product has the same appearance all over the world is not the whole solution.

In addition to the branding issue, cultural issues predominate. Francis Fukuyama, a novelist, summed this up as well as anyone. "International life will be seen increasingly as a competition not between rival ideologies – since most economically successful states will be organized along similar lines – but between different cultures." Investment appraisal and return on investment calculations have cultural differences across the globe. International companies need to build this into their investment appraisal processes, or they will impose unsuitable rules resulting, for example, in subsidiary companies working either too risk-averse, or too gung-ho.

Most individual managers learn about cultural differences the hard way. When I first went to sell British products in America, I started off with an approach that could be summed up as "Unlike my European customers, US businesspeople that I have to deal with predominantly speak English. I will therefore treat them as English people with a funny accent." How wrong could he be?

People experienced in doing business in Europe have a steep learning curve if they are to be successful in the USA and vice versa. Taking a simple example (and a huge generalization), there is a huge difference between how Americans and Europeans treat salespeople. In Europe the starting point of a sales prospect is a sort of growling suspicion, and the salesperson has to work hard to break this down and get the prospect in the first place to neutrality, before moving on to try to make them warm to the sales proposition. In America their attitude is much more welcoming and positive. They will congratulate you on the concept of your product and find as many positive things to say about it as they can. If, however, they actually see no need for it, or are aware of a competitive product they believe to be superior, the salesperson can end up with a totally wrong impression of the seriousness that the American prospect will bring to a consideration of the proposition. Many salespeople from the UK have returned home from prospecting visits to North America promising stupendous orders that never in the end appear.

Now look at it from the opposite point of view. If an American businessperson gets into an airplane and travels from coast to coast, they will be in the aircraft for over five hours. They get out, and find much the same culture as the one they left behind. The same federal laws apply, the education system is very similar and, of course, their native tongue will do nicely. Now put the same American on to an airplane from London to Paris, a 45-minute trip, and they find themselves on what seems to be a different planet. They are much less used than Europeans are to adapting to different cultures.

Now expand your global thinking to include Japan, and the size of the cultural problem becomes massive. Even people who have worked in Japan and with Japanese people for some time still find it difficult to express how Japanese business people operate.

So the question an investor needs to answer to is how well a company is dealing with the cultural or people side of globalization as well as the branding and marketing point of view.

The key to global return on investment is to find the correct level of risk and return that fits the group's strategy modified by local conditions.

A STRATEGY FOR GLOBALIZATION

If you are looking for a benchmark on globalization, one of the most successful exponents has to be Nokia. A Finnish company with any pretensions to growth has, because of the size of its local market, to think globally very early.

Any company building a global brand needs a philosophy whereby subsidiary companies are somehow simultaneously consistent with their global HQ, but also relatively autonomous in making changes, or investments, when it becomes clear that a trend in the domestic market may not work overseas. This is true for any other multinational company, but think how much more true it must be for Nokia. With a tiny market share derived from its home country and ever-shortening product life cycles, it has been critical for Nokia to get the balance right between central control and local culture.

Another crucial aspect of Nokia's brand building across the world lies in moving quickly. Their expansion of production facilities abroad has been very fast, building factories on every continent during a single year.

In a 1998 *Financial Times* article, "Survey Mastering Global Business 4: How subsidiaries can be more than bit players," the business author Karl Moore suggests that in the emerging global economy most subsidiaries have lost strategic decision-making power to their multinational headquarters, while relatively few have gained a larger global role thanks to deliberate decentralization. Many of those centralizing decisions have typically taken control of which markets to compete for, which products to introduce, what type of manager to hire, and where to locate the research and development and manufacturing parts of the firm. While this has cleared the decks for global strategy and global competitive moves, it has often resulted in demotivated subsidiary teams and a considerable drop in overall corporate learning.

An investor needs to look for clues on how well a company is performing in this regard. Look, for example, at the concept of the internal customer, very important when working with other cultures. If a company regards the departments in subsidiary companies as somehow subservient to Head Office, then it has a real problem. If it looks on them as internal customers then it is already half way to understanding their culture and producing the best product for the local market.

For Nokia, the key is dependent on the leadership of subsidiary company managers and the development of world-class competencies no matter what their provenance. For example, Nokia in the UK has built up its R&D capabilities over the years to the point where its facility now has global responsibility for important lines of product.

A GLOBAL KNOWLEDGE CENTER

Possibly the most important aspect of globalization, after branding, is looking at how resources, both capital and expertise, are invested around the world. After all, the opportunities for re-inventing the wheel grow in direct proportion to the number of countries in which an organization operates. To record and communicate experience in return on investment and decision-making you need a global knowledge center with five main components.

Tools

The model this book proposes as the method of calculating return on investment can be a template included in an e-based knowledge center. Teams need to use a consistent methodology and a common business or financial language to improve productivity and communication. The return on investment tool has its place in this, as members of teams build a picture not only of what their colleagues globally are investing in, but more importantly of the thinking that went into making the decision.

E-learning

The availability of best practice concepts and explanations, including, for example, investment appraisal, allows people with access to the knowledge center to use a self-paced learning environment and "learn at the point of doing."

Experts

If, in trying to come to terms with an investment decision, you need help, either with the process or the topic in question, a global knowledge center gives you the names of and access to internal experts in your organization. This facility may include direct contact with the expert or the storage of frequently asked questions and insights.

Forum

Picking up the theme from the Human Resources Director's cry for help that we must pass experience from one project into another, the Forum becomes an important part of the global knowledge center. Here like-minded individuals can discuss their views of the costs, benefits, and risks of a mutually interesting investment opportunity. Useful too in an environment where far-flung teams are working on the same products or customers. For example, a subsidiary in Australia about to invest in production machinery can use the forum to get direct experience of others in the organization who have dealt with the same suppliers of the machinery.

Knowledge base

Building a knowledge base available worldwide depends on growing a series of real-life projects and cases being made available in a database. Taking the narrow example of investment appraisal, the availability and storage in the knowledge base of strategic and financial analysis of investment decisions that are key to your own is a very useful resource. On a wider basis, using consistent tools in many aspects of business processes builds the global database of knowledge that the organization needs to maintain. They say we live in the information age; the problem is to keep information already generated in your organization, and prosper from it. Building real-life cases, with a consistent index for searching purposes, is the way that organizations will eventually solve this problem.

KEY LEARNING POINTS

1 Built into a multi-national investment appraisal system is a balance between central control and local empowerment

2 A robust investment appraisal process, implemented globally, gives a huge opportunity for managers in one part of the world to learn from others

3 They build a library of return on investment calculations and make them available worldwide.

The State of the Art

Take a more holistic view of return on investment by forging a tight link between projects you intend to subject to financial evaluation and your strategy.

» Documenting a business strategy
» Building a business case template
» Using a risk analysis process
» Evaluating projects against the balanced scorecard

"The end product of strategic decisions is deceptively simple; a combination of products and markets is selected for the firm. This combination is arrived at by addition of new product markets, divestment from some old ones, and expansion of the present system."

Igor Ansoff, b.1918, strategy guru

Return on investment or investment appraisal was seen in the past by many organizations as the remit of the finance department. In previous chapters we have seen that the difficulties and opportunities in the topic are, in fact, much more concerned with the management of the whole business. Return on investment of a single project must not only be seen tactically as a cash impact on the business, but must be seen more holistically as a vital part of strategic and forward planning.

In the past we have tended to look at projects as they occur, from an idea from a customer, colleague, or supplier, for example. Nowadays it is part of the strategic planning remit of any functional manager to search for new opportunities to serve existing customers better or create new customers. This is why the words of Ansoff are so useful as the starting point.

There is no such thing as a product unless there is a market for it, and equally there is no such thing as a market unless you have a product to take to it. The "product market" therefore is a key starting point for a strategic plan, and return on investment becomes not a tool only used for evaluating projects, a rather reactive concept, but a proactive tool for looking for advances in strategic product markets. It becomes, in effect, a template for seeking business cases and new projects.

There are five steps in this process:

» use the product market concept to express your strategy;
» build a business-case template;
» use the template to identify new opportunities;
» use the balanced scorecard so that managers test soft data as well as hard; and
» assess the risks of going ahead with a proposal.

We will look at each in turn.

USE THE PRODUCT MARKET CONCEPT TO EXPRESS YOUR STRATEGY

Starting from an analysis of what is happening in your chosen markets, what the competition is doing there, and other external and internal parameters, and with a good understanding of its purpose, a strategic planning team can move to choosing its product markets.

Development priorities and methods

Looking into the future, the organization has a number of alternatives for development, which can best be surmised using an Ansoff matrix (Fig. 6.1).

Products/Services

	Current	New
Current	1	3
New	2	4

Markets

Options include:
withdrawal, consolidation, market penetration,
market development, product development and diversification

Fig. 6.1 Development priorities.

» Cell 1: Here you have three alternatives: withdrawing from the market, sustaining the current provision of products and services to current markets, or increasing the market share or penetration of current markets using existing products and services. Withdrawal may not be pleasant, but if it is required, it had best be done in a planned way!
» Cell 2: This represents the provision of current products and services to new markets – however you currently segment the markets.
» Cell 3: This represents the provision of new products and services to current markets.
» Cell 4: This represents the provision of new products and services to new markets. This is known as diversification. To be successful here

requires significant effort in research and development of sourcing, and sales and markets. Moving into one unknown area is difficult, but to do two simultaneously has proved too difficult even for many of the world's multinationals.

Where development in either direction has been identified, then the organization still has a number of further choices based around:

» internal versus external (make or buy); and
» acquisition, joint-venture, partnership, licensing etc.

Indeed, the thinking still needs to flow freely at this stage. If the plan is to be creative, it must not be held back by, for example, what already exists.

The way ahead clear; it is time in planning terms to make some decisions on what products you are going to sell. Probably the most important activity so far, this exercise has to be done at all levels, and agreed by all the line managers concerned.

In deciding what products and services to offer, or what markets and customers to focus on, the organization should identify what criteria drive performance. This, as we will see, is also the starting point of the next step in the return on investment process, building a business template.

Some criteria will be mandatory, such as complying with legislation; others will be more subjective, maximizing profitability for example, with no clear definition of numerical objectives at this stage. The subjective criteria are not all equally important and should therefore be weighted. A simple scale of 1–10 will probably sort out the priorities.

This list of criteria will be used in the formulation of strategy to help prioritize product market combinations in the activity matrix that follows. However, once identified, they should be circulated to everybody in the organization as they can be used to assess every decision made in all functions and at all levels. They represent the first step in holistic return on investment, where an organization attempts to connect its strategy to its tactical system of comparing projects or opportunities.

Activity matrix

The activity matrix is a two-dimensional matrix which maps product and service "groupings" against market segments or groupings.

To achieve the matrix, the first step is to segment each category into logical groupings which should be able to contain 100% of all current and future product/market combinations.

In this way it will be possible to plot the current picture against the future picture, and thereby show the degree of change in the organization's operations over the period of the analysis.

Grouping should recognize the difference in the capability needs or financing requirements or degree of change in both products and markets. Some markets have different servicing requirements due to geographic location, size, complexity, channel etc., and some products have different requirements as measured by technology, stage of life cycle, manufacturing needs, etc.

A simple example that might help to show the value of such a matrix is given in Fig. 6.2.

Markets & Customers

	Group A	Group B	Group C
Group A	H > L	M > L	Not applicable
Group B	M > H	0 > M	0 > M

Products/services

Fig. 6.2 The activity matrix.

In each cell, the current emphasis (graded H = high, M = medium, L = low and 0 = zero) is shown on the left, with the future emphasis on the right. A completed matrix should contain a maximum of 100 cells at a strategic level, and there should be no more than 25% as high emphasis as this may reflect a lack of focus.

What strategy, then, does this diagram represent?

» Market group A is more important than Group B but this will change in the future.
» Both product groups A and B are important now and in the future.
» Significant sales and marketing activity will be required to develop the sales of product group B to market group B.
» Resource commitment (people, effort, money, and so on) will be moved from market group A to market group B.

For each product market cell, where the planning team has identified either high or medium future emphasis, the key success factors should be clearly understood – this is sometimes called the "basis of competition," as the attributes used by customers when making purchasing decisions represent the bases on which organizations compete for business.

The connection between the two diagrams will also be clear, as the planners use the development priorities to define the product/markets.

Performance expectations

Emphasis areas within the matrix are identified using the H, M, L classifications – reflecting the current and anticipated levels of activity in each cell, and hence the name "activity matrix."

At the strategic level the use of H, M, L is probably sufficient. However, for planning purposes and to move towards return on investment calculations, more work is required.

These letters should be translated into hard and tangible performance data – revenue, profit, budget, people, capital equipment investment etc. (whatever is meaningful for the organization).

Planning analysts or functional experts can raise the activity matrix, but the information should come back to the top of the organization as it provides an excellent first "validation" of their strategic thinking. The "mix" is also important, as it will show the overall percentage coming from one product grouping, or from a particular market grouping. This gives the organization an insight into risk or dependency on particular areas. You can use the mix and degree of change over time for each function to evaluate the appropriate budget and allocation.

Once figures have been placed in each cell "from the bottom up" this will provide an aggregation consistent with overall performance expectations of the whole organization.

BUILD A BUSINESS-CASE TEMPLATE

Once you have built and agreed your strategic plan, using the Ansoff matrix or not, the next step in the process is to communicate it widely to everyone who may at some point present a business case with a calculation of return on investment. It will not last for ever of course, but until your next review it remains the starting point for management as they set objectives within it and build operational plans.

In order to check how well activities that you have got going at the moment fit in with the strategy, you now build a business template. Having assessed current activities you can then use the same template to look for the strategic fit of future plans and projects.

To create the template, list the most important criteria of your strategy. These may be about timescales, for example, with importance given to short-term sales. Or they might be about cashflow such as a criterion that any activity should be cash positive within one year. Give each criterion a rating out of 10, reflecting its importance to the strategy. 0 means of little impact on the strategy, and 10 means a very significant impact on the strategy. To test an existing or a new idea, think about how you would define the ideal for each criterion. For example, if the criterion is to keep staff to a minimum, the ideal might be that the new idea reduces the number of staff. If a proposal maintains the number of staff in these circumstances you would give a medium rating to the idea against this criterion. If it reduced staff numbers it would get a high rating and if it required more staff it would get a very low rating. Rate the new idea against each of the criteria according to how close it comes to the ideal, and multiply this rating by the weighting. Ideally, of course, the new idea would score 10 against each criterion, so calculate what that would be as a benchmark for each idea. Add up the two scores to give you the total ideal and actual ratings and then express it as a percentage.

In the example in Fig. 6.3 a new idea is measured against three criteria. It scores well against the first and third, but not so well against the second. Added together, the weighted scores give a total figure that is translated into a percentage. With 61%, this idea has a reasonable strategic fit, and its originator may very well want to go to the next stage of calculating the return on investment knowing that they will not be blindsided by senior managers declaring the project non-strategic.

Criterion	Priority	New idea	Weighting	Ideal Weighting
Increase short term sales	7	7	49	70
Protect long term sales	5	2	10	50
Keep staff to minimum	7	8	56	70
Total scores			115	190
Percentage of ideal				61%

Fig. 6.3 Example of a business template in use.

USE THE TEMPLATE TO IDENTIFY NEW OPPORTUNITIES

It is a rather depressing fact that a lot of middle managers complain that the board of their company or division does not have a strategy. Since this is one of the Board's most important responsibilities, it seems unlikely that this will be the case, at least not in such numbers as managers have reported to me over the years. What they are really saying is that the Board has not communicated or handed down the strategy in a way that managers could understand and build into their operating plans. The communication has to go both ways. Managers are more likely to work within a strategy if they helped to devise it than if it came down on tablets of stone. But, of course, it is a balance.

Everyone recognizes that there is the time for a strong lead and a time for consensus building. If there is a revolution in one of the countries where your product plant is based, or a fire at a warehouse, it is not the time to call a focus group and find consensus. Equally, if you want to take bright engineers with you in terms of your strategy development, the way not to do it is to arrive at a planning meeting knowing that the only acceptable plan is inside the head of the senior person present. That's a waste of time for everyone.

The balance is to get things done by taking a dictatorial approach when necessary but wherever possible seeking opinions and consulting, particularly when the key to success is motivating people to buy into a strategy to achieve a vision. One of the practitioners of using business templates is the telecommunications company Nokia. It is able to use such templates because of its policy on strategy and the communication of strategy.

It is Nokia practice to announce a strategy change to a group of individuals and then for that group immediately to consult with the next level down on the implications of the change for them. What this means is that everyone recognizes their involvement in how the company is managed while recognizing that in the end decisions have to be made, sometimes very fast owing to the nature of the business.

Trevor Merriden writes in his book *Business the Nokia Way*[1], "Phil Brown, head of Nokia Mobile Phones' UK marketing and sales division, talks about the speed with which strategy is passed down the management structure. This is essential because on a broad subject like the global information society, different parts of Nokia have to develop their own versions of the strategy. There are checks and balances, such as the company scorecard mechanism (see below), which are designed to see whether the overall objective of the company is being translated into specific goals further down the company. But the important thing in terms of leadership style is that managers are allowed to deliver the message in their own way. The manager must achieve results, but he is considered in the first instance to be best placed to deliver the message so as to achieve these results."

So, given that managers understand the company's strategy and how it impacts their part of the business, they can move to using the business template to test the ideas they and their people are coming up with, and as a thought starter for searching for other new ideas.

Managers should encourage their teams to use the business template as a matter of course. A starting point for this might be to challenge what they are doing now with the template. If they have a process in place, or are allocating resources in the wrong place, the business template should alert them to this. Adopting this logical process for assessing current and new plans encourages team members to view issues objectively. The more the business template is used, the more experienced the team will become at evaluating suggestions. Additionally, once team members realize exactly what the criteria and ideals are, they will be more likely to make suggestions that come close to those important requirements.

Just before we move on, it is worth pointing out that not all the data used to explain how well a project meets the template criteria will be internal. For example, a salesforce will often be able to explain how an idea that they are suggesting will meet a criterion of producing short-term sales; they just need to refer to their customers. To prove the long-term opportunity may require them to refer to gurus, technical journals, and the experience of other people.

USE THE BALANCED SCORECARD SO THAT MANAGERS TEST SOFT DATA AS WELL AS HARD

State of the art companies are looking at themselves and return on investment in a more comprehensive way than simply looking at their figures. Shareholders also are thinking about business more holistically, taking a broader look at its activities to assess its long-term future.

The management gurus Kaplan and Norton advocate the concept of investment appraisal and, incidentally in the management accounting policies that chart historical progress as well, of the balanced scorecard. This requires the system to give information in four different areas, each answering a different question.

1 Customers: "How do they see us?"
2 Internal: "What must we excel at?"
3 Financial: "How do shareholders see us?"
4 Innovation: "How can we continue to learn, improve, and add value?"

The key idea of the balanced scorecard is that a business, and therefore its managers, has a responsibility for more than just *profits*. Here is another expression of the same concept.

Managers are also responsible for the level of *customer service* they offer. This is true whether the customers are external, in terms of people who pay cash for products and services, or internal, where a service is provided within the business by, for example, the Information Technology department to the rest of the business.

They also have to meet a series of *quality* targets concerned with reliability, competitiveness, and innovation.

Finally, they have to operate with some form of *environment* targets. All companies are required to work within legal environmental constraints; many are keeping a step ahead of the regulations and doing their bit for the planet.

The headings in each topic could be as follows, and management may care to set operating targets as well as strategic targets for each of them as an adjunct to the business template. This forces managers putting up new ideas to check each element of the balanced scorecard that is important to their organization. An example of a balanced scorecard is shown in Fig. 6.4.

There are as many ways to present business cases and management accounts as there are companies. It is advisable occasionally to take a step back and reconsider whether your current way of evaluating and reporting is still the best way. Having passed both of these strategic tests, the business template and the balanced scorecard, managers can move through the more traditional methods of calculating return on investment.

A RISK ANALYSIS TOOL

Modern thinking about risk management has its place in return on investment calculation. I would pick out as state of the art the measuring of risk across an organization in a consistent way and the storing of previous analysis. This means that other people in the organization at a later date can benefit from the work that previous teams have done. A senior human resources director in a telecommunications company recently said to me: "The most important problem facing the design and production teams of this organization is the fact that we never learn from one project to another. This risk assessment tool is a very simple analytical tool, but stored and made accessible to others could be worth its weight in gold."

An example of the form that the team needs to fill in to identify and assess the risks of a investment decision is given in Fig. 6.5.

Profits	Customer service
Measured by:	Measured by:
Division	Delivery dates
Product	Complaints
Service	Business processes
Market region	Activity levels
Age of product	Time to repair
Bought in/built here	Mean time between failures
Quality	**Environment**
Measured by:	Measured by:
Strategic innovation	Raw materials used
Product innovation	Packaging type and amount
Competitiveness	Supplier compliance
Returns	Energy used
Warranty repairs	Waste and recycling
Reliability	Pollution

Fig. 6.4 Example of a balanced scorecard.

Risk analysis is one of those processes that is very difficult to do on your own. Let us assume that there is a team looking at an investment decision.

The first column is an identifier for reference purposes. The second identifies the nature of the risk. Ask the team, "What are the potential

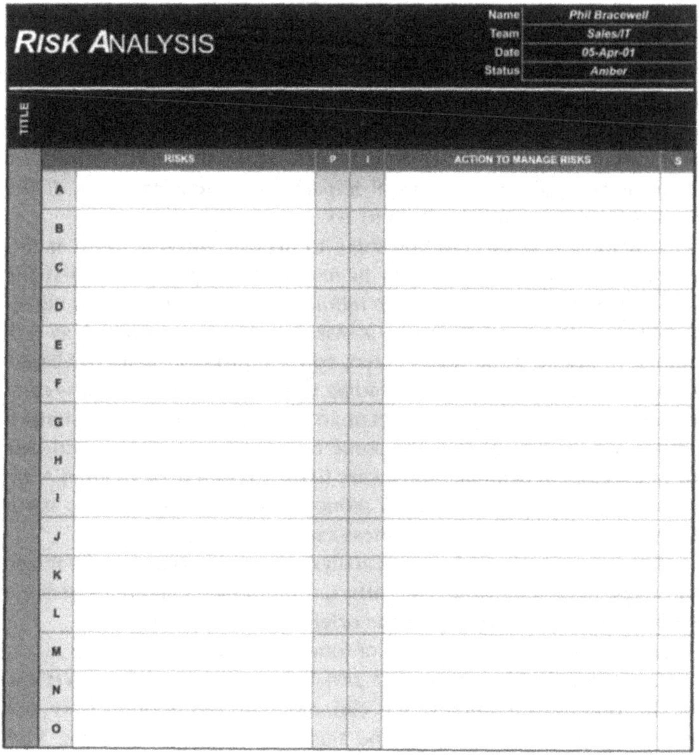

RISK ANALYSIS

Name	Phil Bracewell
Team	Sales/IT
Date	05-Apr-01
Status	Amber

TITLE

	RISKS	P	I	ACTION TO MANAGE RISKS	S
A					
B					
C					
D					
E					
F					
G					
H					
I					
J					
K					
L					
M					
N					
O					

Fig. 6.5 Risk assessment form.

problems associated with this activity or project? What could go wrong?" As a memory jogger or thought starter, the team might care to use the groupings "What could go wrong financially?" "What could go wrong technically?" and "What could go wrong practically?" Since the last of these includes those aspects of performance that involve people changing how they do things, it is likely to be a large area of risk.

The third column marked "P" is the team's intuitive feel for how likely it is that the risk will happen. Mark 10 if the chances of occurrence are more or less a certainty, and down to 1 where the risk is very unlikely to occur. Some risks have more impact on performance than others. Identify these by marking in the "I" column the impact that the risk will have on performance or achievement of the decision's objectives. If the impact is low, a marginal impact only, then mark it 1. If the impact is significant, mark it up to 10.

Now look at what could be done to manage the risk. Look at this in two ways: what you can do to minimize the probability that the risk will occur, and how you can minimize the impact if it does occur. Finally, use the "S" column to assess the status of each risk as red, amber, or green. If the status is red, you will probably want to change something in the project plan, leading to a change in the business case, either to a lower level of benefits or an increase in costs. If the status is amber, you may want to move some benefits from the expected case to a best case, or from the worst case to the expected, or you may want to put in additional contingency money on the costs side. If the status is green, you will leave the business case as it stands.

When should you perform risk analysis? Certainly as part of the return on investment calculation, but also during implementation whenever something changes that alters the original business case.

Figure 6.6 shows an example of four risks as a diagram.

Those risks with low impact and low probability of occurrence, in the bottom left corner, we can more or less forget. They will not in all probability impact the business case. Those in the high probability but low impact quarter, bottom right, you will look at in terms of assessing whether or not it is worthwhile trying to prevent the occurrence, or whether you should change the business case. In the top left corner, where the impact is high but the probability low, we should look for ways to protect ourselves against occurrence and mitigate the impact if they do occur. However, that mitigation will probably affect the business case. The overwhelming focus for action, though, is those risks that lie in the top right hand quarter, where the probability is high and so is the impact. You must change the business case significantly or put in place a convincing plan to prevent the risk occurring.

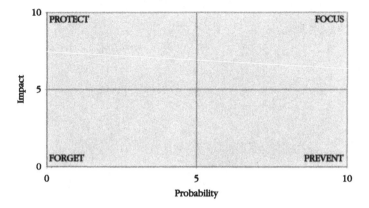

Fig. 6.6   Risk diagram.

KEY LEARNING POINTS

1 Return on investment has to be seen as part of a holistic approach to the management of an organization or a team.
2 Building a template for business cases flowing from your strategy gives you a powerful weapon for testing your current activities.
3 Building such a template also gives you an opportunity to searching for new projects that will have a tight strategic fit.
4 You can then go into the investment appraisal process to check the tactical financial case.
5 Risk analysis nowadays is a company-wide technique, where consistency and making previous experience available to other managers play their part in reducing risk and increasing return.

NOTE

1 Merriden, T. (2000) *Business the Nokia Way*. Capstone, Oxford.

In Practice: Three Examples

Three case studies, two of them concerning business decisions and one concerned with investors calculating return on their portfolios.

» Do we start a new service for our customers?
» Do we stay in an existing product market?
» Using the DCF technique to determine shareholder return

"The proof of the pudding is in the eating."

Fourteenth-century proverb

The three case studies I have chosen to illustrate the theory of investment appraisal concern an oil company. Because the figures arise as a result of internal work using actual numbers, I am unable for commercial confidentiality reasons to use anything but the fictional name OCC Plc. If you have in mind any of the large oil companies that operate globally, you will have the right type of company in mind. In the first example we look at an opportunity the IT department of the company at Head Office had to put in place a disaster recovery system to service some internal departments, and that they could sell to other organizations as a service.

The second concerns the telecommunications department's examination of the current service it supplies to its internal customers, in order to work out whether they should reinvest in the business or withdraw from it as providing an insufficient return.

The third is the use of the discounted cashflow technique to measure return on investment of a portfolio of shares.

STARTING A NEW IT SERVICE

In this example an IT director is trying to cost justify purchasing the equipment and doing the work to offer a new service to his customers, who include the various departments of OCC Plc, the oil company which he works for, and some external prospects. He puts each potential customer into one of four groups depending on the likelihood of their placing an order for the new service. He then makes an estimate of the likely income stream over the next three years allowing for the fact that there may be delays in departments and prospects taking the service up (see Table 7.1).

From this he can calculate three possibilities for the total stream. This will be the basis for the projected profit and loss account he needs to raise to start the business case. The pessimistic case assumes that only the prospects in likelihood 1 will place an order. The most likely case adds the prospects in likelihood 2, and the optimistic case assumes all the prospects will come on board (see Table 7.2).

Table 7.1

	Prospect	Year 1	Years 2 and 3
Likelihood 1	Interohm (External)	112.5	150
	Large Gty Bank (External)	162	324
	Technical Dept	90	120
	Research Dept	64.8	86.4
	Engineering Division	36	48
	Chemicals Division	0	86.4
Total Likelihood 1		465.3	814.8
Likelihood 2	Ranters (External)	112.5	150
	Finance Dept	64.8	86.4
	Minerals Division	24	48
Total Likelihood 2		201.3	284.4
Likelihood 3	Oil Division	90	120
	GPD	36	48
Total Likelihood 3		126	168
Likelihood 0	Detergent Division	36	48

Table 7.2

Year	1	2	3
Pessimistic (likelihood 1)	465.3	814.8	814.8
Most likely (likelihood 1+2)	666.6	1,099.2	1,099.2
Optimistic (likelihood 1+2+3)	792.6	1,267.2	1,267.2

OCC management do not like projects that require the optimistic forecasts of benefits in order to make a convincing business case. We only need, then, to produce the profit and loss accounts for the most likely outcome and the pessimistic. In the profit and loss account we will allow for depreciation of the fixed asset over the three-year life of the project. The accountants have told us to handle depreciation as follows. The capital costs of 1711 should be spread over the three years, but they have agreed that there will be a residual value of the equipment at the end of that time. This value they have allowed to be

15%. Depreciation is therefore the total cost of the asset minus 15%, divided over the three years.

Given that, Tables 7.3 and 7.4 show what the two profit and loss accounts will look like.

Table 7.3 Projected profit and loss account based on most likely income.

Year	1	2	3
Expenditure			
Staff	70.0	70.0	70.0
Maintenance	0.0	35.0	35.0
Depreciation	485.0	485.0	486.0
Accommodation	18.0	18.0	18.0
Electricity	15.0	15.0	15.0
Sundries	43.0	43.0	43.0
Total	631.0	666.0	667.0
Income	666.6	1,099.2	1,099.2
Profit	35.6	433.2	432.2
Cashflow	520.6	918.2	918.2

Table 7.4 Projected profit and loss account based on pessimistic income.

Year	1	2	3
Expenditure (as before)	631.0	666.0	667.0
Income	465.3	814.8	814.8
Profit	−165.7	148.8	147.8
Cashflow	319.3	633.8	633.8

The profit and loss account does not contain any contingency money for costs. The reason for this is that the risks in predicting the income stream so far outweigh any possible additional expenditure on the cost side that it renders it irrelevant. We will judge this project on the likelihood of the income stream providing a viable business. Notice how we have converted the profit and loss into a cashflow at the end. The only difference between the two in this example is depreciation, which is added back to the bottom line to give the cashflow. The capital will be spent before the start of the process, and we will look after that in the last step of the investment appraisal process.

To maintain realism our discounted cashflow must take account of the tax liability that will arise. You always need the accountants to help with such a calculation. Every company is different and the tax treatment of such a project is hard to predict if you are an accountant closely involved with the company's tax position and impossible if you are not.

In this case we have been told to use a tax rate of 35%. Where there is a positive cashflow it comes through to the company as an addition to profits. Such profits are, of course, taxable. In cashflow terms the cash implications of tax occur the year after the liability, since they occur after the end of the company year when the company has worked out its profits and the tax implications. So, since the project has a positive cashflow in Year 1 of £521, it will have a cash outflow for tax in Year 2 of 35% of £521 − £182.

There is one further tax complication. The capital expenditure for this project is £1,711 (always working in £000's) and the way that is treated for tax is different. No matter how a company's accountants and auditors decide to treat depreciation for profit and loss account purposes, the tax authorities have their own method. So far we have talked about the straight-line method of depreciation where an asset is depreciated by a fixed amount in each of the years of its usefulness. The tax authorities use another method called reducing balance. With this method the asset is depreciated by a set percentage each year with the balance carried forward to the next year. In this case the initial value of the asset is £1,711. This is reduced by 25% of the reducing balance each year. So, 25% of £1,711 is £428 and the tax rate of 35% therefore gives a tax benefit in Year 2 of £149.8, rounded up in the cashflow to £150. The value carried forward is £1,711 minus £428 which is £1,283. 25% of that figure is £321 and 35% of that is £112. At the end of Year 3 the asset is sold and tax is allowed at 35% on the difference between the proceeds £257 and the tax written-down value of £962.

Notice how you require Year 4 to take into account the tax payments, even although the project is being measured over three years (see Tables 7.5 and 7.6).

Table 7.5 Cashflow forecast: most likely outcome.

Year	0	1	2	3	4
Capital	(1,711)			257	
Tax capital allowances			150	112	247
Operating cashflow		521	918	918	
Tax			(182)	(321)	(321)
Cashflow	(1,711)	521	886	966	(74)
Discount factors 7%	1	0.93	0.87	0.82	0.76
Present value	(1,711)	484	771	792	(57)
Net present value	**£279**				
Written down value		1,711	1,283	962	
Capital allowance		428	321		
Balancing allowance				705	

Table 7.6 Cashflow forecast: pessimistic outcome.

Year	0	1	2	3	4
Capital	(1,711)			257	
Tax capital allowances			150	112	247
Operating cashflow		319	634	634	
Tax			(112)	(222)	(222)
Cashflow	(1,711)	319	672	781	25
Discount factors 7%	1	0.93	0.87	0.82	0.76
Present value	(1,711)	297	584	641	19
Net present value	**(£170)**				
Written down value		1,711	1,283	962	
Capital allowance		428	321		
Balancing allowance				705	

The NPV for the pessimistic outcome is negative at £(170), while that for the most likely is positive at £279. The main difference between the two cashflows are the customers with the likelihood of 2. There are a number of things we can do about this. We can go back to the main likelihood 2 prospects and try and close them off in one way or another. Either get them to sign up or at least appear much more positive about signing up, or cross them off the list. The removal of uncertainty greatly increases the chances of making a good decision. Putting resource into these prospects may involve removing it from the likelihood 3 candidates. But this is no problem because we can get to a viable project without them and maybe come to see them as the icing on the cake once the project has been implemented and successful to the most likely estimate.

DO WE STAY IN THE BUSINESS OR GET OUT?

An oil company Central Information Systems (CIS) manager has to decide whether to upgrade the telephone equipment they use to provide a telephony service or come out of the business.

The company, OCC Plc, has four headquarters buildings in a premier site in the City of London. There is £2,600,000 worth of capital cost for a new telephone exchange (PABX) and a large amount of peripheral equipment that OCC intend to rent.

In this illustration I have left in the detail so that, if you would like to, you can work through the detailed accountancy part as well as the end-product cashflows.

The CIS Manager gets the following information from the telephone manager.

OCC PLC

From: Telephone Manager
To: CIS Manager

Existing telephone arrangements

I enclose the Year 1 budget for the existing telephone system. According to the recent survey, the usage of the system if we fail to upgrade it will be as shown in Table 7.7.

Table 7.7

Year	1	2	3	4	5
No of users	5,500	3,900	2,500	1,000	500

In terms of increase, the number of calls is proportional to the number of users, we find, and we charge £340 per user for rental. The rest I think is self-explanatory.

Proposed new system

This much we have agreed. The capital cost is £2,600,000. Rental charges for user equipment will be a fixed rate £120,000 in a full year and maintenance is free for Year 1, £80,000 for Year 2, £100,000 thereafter subject to inflation.

Our ability to charge rental to the user will not change but it is certain that there will be an increase in usage of the equipment given the new facilities available. I have got an estimate of increased usage from one of the major customers. Another major benefit of the new system is that directory charges will be part of the telephone system as opposed to the separate computer system we are charged for now.

I am looking forward to our meeting when I hope you can help me to produce the numbers for the new system. Some of the assumptions I have got are mine and I understand them, the others are from finance and I'm not so sure. The budgeted profit and loss account for Year 1 is shown in Fig. 7.1.

Notes on the Do nothing scenario

1 The Year 1 figures are the existing budget for the division.
2 Staff costs in that budget include salary costs, NI, pension and other benefits.
3 Staff numbers are expected to reduce in line with usage. All elements of staff costs are expected to increase at 8% p.a.
4 The number of calls made is proportional to the number of users. The cost per unit is expected to increase at 6% p.a. Users are charged cost + 2% for calls.

Do nothing scenario

Budgeted profit and loss account for year 1

Expenditure	£000's
Staff	217
Equipment maintenance	160
Equipment rental	114
Depreciation	0
Accommodation	316
Directory	230
Calls	1,617
Management overheads	282
Total costs	2,936

Income	
Calls	1,649
Rental	1,870
Total income	3,519
Profit	583

Fig. 7.1 Budgeted profit and loss account for Year 1.

5 Management overheads will be charged at 8% of income throughout the period.
6 Rental per user in Year 1 is £340 per unit. This charge is expected to increase at 6% p.a.
7 Current equipment rental charges are fixed by contract until the end of Year 3. Thereafter they will reduce in line with the number of users. Rate will not change.
8 Maintenance costs in Year 1 consist of labor and material costs in equal amounts. Materials used reduce in line with usage of the

system. However, the reducing amount of materials bought will result in the loss from Year 2 onwards of a 10% discount previously enjoyed on all such purchases. Also, because of the increasing obsolescence of these materials, they will suffer price inflation of 8% p.a.

9 Labor costs consist of five individuals in Year 1. It will be possible to move these individuals to other parts of the company as their maintenance work becomes unnecessary. These moves will save the company from recruiting other staff.

10 Directory costs will reduce in line with the number of users and are subject to rate inflation of 6%.

11 Accommodation costs increase at 6% p.a. No space can be freed up as users reduce.

Figure 7.2 shows the profit and loss account if they did nothing. Figure 7.3 shows the profit and loss account if they were to go ahead and buy the new system.

Notes on the New system scenario

1 The Year 1 figures are the existing budget for the division except as noted below.

2 Staff numbers are expected to remain constant.

3 All elements of staff costs are expected to increase at 8% p.a.

4 The number of users will remain the same as at present but the usage of the system is expected to increase by 5% in 1996 and a further 5% in Year 3 as a result of the improved facilities. The cost per unit is expected to increase at 6% p.a. Users are charged cost + 2% for calls.

5 Management overheads will be charged at 8% of income throughout the period.

6 Rental per user in Year 1 is £340 per unit. This charge is expected to increase at 6% p.a.

7 Equipment rental charges for the new system are fixed by contract from the middle of Year 1 until the end of Year 5 at a cost of £120,000.

8 Maintenance costs of the new system in Year 1 are part of the capital cost. In Year 2, a special rate of £80,000 is available. From

Do nothing scenario

Projected profit and loss account

Year	1	2	3	4	5
Expenditure					
Staff	217	166	115	50	27
Equipment maintenance	160	137	103	40	33
Equipment rental	114	114	114	21	10
Depreciation	0	0	0	0	0
Accommodation	316	335	335	376	399
Directory	230	173	117	50	26
Calls	1,617	1,215	826	350	186
Management overheads	282	212	144	61	32
	2,936	2,352	1,774	948	713
Income					
Calls	1,649	1,239	843	357	190
Rental	1,870	1,406	955	405	215
	3,519	2,645	1,798	762	405
Profit	583	293	24	−186	−308

Fig. 7.2 Do nothing scenario: projected profit and loss account.

Year 3 the supplier will provide maintenance at an initial cost of £100,000, inflating at 5%. The old system will need maintaining throughout Year 1.

9 Directory costs in Year 1 will reduce by 40% compared with the original budget. There will be no directory costs thereafter.

New system

Projected profit and loss account

Year	1	2	3	4	5
Expenditure					
Staff	217	234	253	273	295
Add labour	150				
Equipment maintenance	160	80	100	105	110
Equipment rental	60	120	120	120	120
Rental (old system)	114	114	114	0	0
Depreciation	260	520	520	520	520
Accommodation	316	184	195	207	219
Directory	138	0	0	0	0
Calls	1,617	1,800	2,003	2,123	2,251
Management overheads	282	305	332	351	373
	3,314	3,357	3,637	3,699	3,888
Income					
Calls	1,649	1,836	2,043	2,165	2,296
Rental	1,870	1,982	2,101	2,227	2,361
	3,519	3,818	4,144	4,392	4,657
Profit	205	461	507	693	769

Fig. 7.3 New system scenario: projected profit and loss account.

10 Accommodation costs increase at 6% per sq. foot p.a. Space can be freed up at the start of Year 2 to reduce area occupied by 45%.
11 The capital cost of the new system is £2,600,000. This will be incurred at the start of Year 1. However, since the exchange will

not be fully operational until Year 2, depreciation in Year 1 will be restricted to half a year's charge. The system will be sold at the end of Year 5 for its book value.

12 In order to convert to the new system, additional labor costs of £150,000 will be incurred in Year 1.

In Figure 7.4 we can calculate the net present value of the new system proposal by using an incremental cashflow. We could equally well do two cashflows, one for the do nothing scenario and one for buying the new system, but it is common to present the cashflows in this way.

Incremental cashflow

Year		1	2	3	4	5	6
Net cashflow:							
	Existing	583	293	24	−186	−308	
	New system	465	981	1,207	1,213	1,289	
	Incremental cashflow	−118	688	1,003	1,399	1,597	
	Tax		41	−241	−351	−490	−559
	Capital					260	
WDA's/Ball all		228	171	128	96	197	
Net cashflow	−118	957	933	1,176	1,463	−362	
Discount factor	0.87	0.76	0.66	0.57	0.5	0.43	
Present value	−103	727	616	670	731	−156	

Net present value: £2,485 − £2,600 = £(115)

Fig. 7.4   New system scenario: incremental cashflow.

If the rental of the old system is left out of the calculations then cashflow will be £114 higher in Years 1-3, tax will be £40 lower in Years 2-4. The NPV becomes +£67.

£2,485 is the total of the discounted cashflows and £2,600 the initial investment.

£197 is the sum of writing off the £822,656 remaining and subtracting tax due on the £260.

MORE ABOUT RISK ANALYSIS

We have had a look at risk analysis in terms of weighting the likelihood of benefits occurring and costs being overrun. There are a number of useful techniques at this later stage in the process where we use the cashflows created to assess further risk.

Sensitivity analysis

Having gone through the process of understanding the rules and raising your profit and loss account and cashflow, you, the prospective project owner, get further benefits. At this stage you know whether, using the hurdle rate set as a company norm, your project is viable. You also know how it matches up to alternative ways of spending the money - an NPV of $41mn is better than one of $38mn. Now you can use the cashflow for sensitivity analysis or asking the "what if?" question. To be more precise, we can take each uncertainty in the inputs and ask the questions:

1 What is the effect on the NPV if this input changes?
2 How far can the input change before the NPV falls to zero?

In the telephony service example the manager needs to test the discounted cashflow against its sensitivity to the number of users of the new system. We have created a discounted cashflow using the number 5,500 as the number of users. If we had the cashflow on a spreadsheet we could find out what the NPV would be if there were in fact 5,400 users. Similarly, we could find out the number of users we could drop to before the NPV goes negative. We are testing the model for its sensitivity to this parameter, and could repeat the exercise for any parameter on the costs or benefits side.

Using sensitivity analysis helps to identify whether the project is likely to go wrong because of its sensitivity to key inputs. It also tells management which are the key inputs and therefore the ones to be most closely watched once the project is implemented.

Expected value analysis

In this technique, each variable is given a range of possible values with associated probabilities. We might decide that the number of users of the new exchange is not certain to be 5,500 but that there is only a 60% chance of this number being correct. Let us suppose that there is a 40% chance of the number of users being 4,800. The NPV of each outcome has been calculated as shown in Table 7.8.

Table 7.8   Expected value analysis.

No of users	NPV (x)	Probability (p)	xp
4,800	60,444	0.4	24,178
5,500	684,248	0.6	410,549
Expected value: 434,727			

This expected value is simply the weighted average of the separate outcomes. If the project to introduce a new telephone system was undertaken 1,000 times then we would expect the demand to be 4,800 on approximately 400 occasions and 5,500 on approximately 600 occasions. The average return would be the figure quoted above.

You can see from this explanation that this approach is not likely to be very helpful for a capital project that is only undertaken once. The resulting expected value will never actually occur; one of the outcomes in the NPV column will occur – but we don't know which.

If you have trouble with the above consider the average family size in Europe. We could say that the average number of children in a family is 2.2. This average is simply not useful in predicting how many children any household will have. Indeed, we can be absolutely certain that no household will have the average.

So when is expected value useful? Companies use it when they face the same decision over and over again.

Optimistic/most likely/pessimistic estimates

We have seen this method in assessing benefits. Here it is again at the end of the process. Management are asked to make three predictions for each input – an optimistic prediction, a most likely outcome, and a pessimistic prediction. The NPV on each set of assumptions is then computed.

Table 7.9 shows a way of applying this technique to the telephony decision.

Table 7.9 Optimistic/most likely/pessimistic estimates.

Input	Optimistic	Most likely	Pessimistic
No. of users	6,000	5,500	4,500
Mark-up on calls	4%	2%	1%
Staff cost inflation	6%	8%	11%
Rental per user Increase	+10%	0	−5%
NPV	**£1,785,197**	**£684,248**	**£−498,196**

This method can be used on its own – in which case management have an idea of the likely limits to the returns. Alternatively, it can be combined with the expected value analysis method, when probabilities are allocated to each set of assumptions and a single expected value is worked out.

INDIVIDUAL SHARE PERFORMANCE – INCOME AND CAPITAL GAINS

The true return that a shareholder gets from a share is actually quite difficult to identify. Indeed, there was a famous Investment Club in the USA run by the women of a village that was held up as proving that amateurs could beat the professionals at choosing the shares to go into a portfolio because of the very high rate of return. They were only heroines for a while, though, just until someone worked out that they were adding the monthly subscriptions they put in each year as being part of the portfolio's growth!

To get a true comparison of the performance of shares, it is necessary to take into account how much was invested, what the dividend income has been, and most importantly when the transactions took place. If you compared two shares one of which had doubled in price and the other gone up by only 20% you would get the wrong answer if you were unaware that the first share had been held for 10 years and the second for ten weeks.

The only way to track this is to use something like the form in Figure 7.5.

Explanation of the investment record

This record will be cumbersome if you try to keep it manually. It is of course possible, but the record has to have a monthly entry for as long as the share is held. The calculation, after say two years of holding the share, still requires the information on when the original purchase was made.

The heading information gives the name of the company, the type of shares, the year-end and the usual dates of dividend payments.

» Columns 1 and 2: The year and month.
» Columns 3–6: The various types of share transactions.
» Column 7: Balance of shares held at the end of the month. This is calculated as Columns 3 plus 4 plus 5 minus 6.
» Column 8: Cost incurred this month. In the example the shareholder bought 284 shares in an OCC Plc in November of Year 2. This was their total holding at the end of the month. Further costs will only occur if more money is invested at a later date.
» Column 9: The amount of dividends paid, which is noted in the appropriate month.
» Column 10: This allows for the fact that investors may choose to reduce a holding in shares as well as increase it. Obviously, money gained from the proceeds of sales is recorded and kept by date. This

Investment record

Name of company	OCC Plc
Type of share	Ord 25p
Year ends	December
Usual date of interim dividend	Feb May
Usual date of final dividend	Aug Nov

Year	Date	Number of shares bought	Bonus issue shares	Rights issues shares	Number of shares sold	Balance held	Month cost	Dividends	Proceeds from sales	Mid price per share	Selling price	Net selling value	Monthly c/f	DCF	Annualized
2	Nov	284				284	1,346.16				£0.00	£0.00	£1,346.16		
	Feb					284					£0.00	£0.00	£0.00		
3	Jan					284					£0.00	£0.00	£11.36		
	Dec					284		£11.36			£0.00	£0.00	£0.00		
	Mar					284					£0.00	£0.00	£0.00		
	Apr					284					£0.00	£0.00	£0.00		
	May					284		12.07			£0.00	£0.00	£12.07		
	Jun					284					£0.00	£0.00	£0.00		
	Jul					284					£0.00	£0.00	£0.00		
	Aug					284		12.07			£0.00	£0.00	£12.07		
	Sep					284					£0.00	£0.00	£0.00		
	Oct					284					£0.00	£0.00	£0.00		
	Nov					284		14.20			£0.00	£0.00	£14.20		
	Dec					284					£0.00	£0.00	£0.00		
	Jan					284					£0.00	£0.00	£0.00		
4	Feb					284		14.20		6.84	£6.67	£1,894.00	£1,908.20	2.57%	35.53%
	Mar					284					£0.00	£0.00	£0.00		
	Apr					284					£0.00	£0.00	£0.00		
	May					284					£0.00	£0.00	£0.00		
	Jun					284					£0.00	£0.00	£0.00		
	Jul					284					£0.00	£0.00	£0.00		
	Aug					284					£0.00	£0.00	£0.00		
	Sep					284					£0.00	£0.00	£0.00		
	Oct					284					£0.00	£0.00	£0.00		
	Nov					284					£0.00	£0.00	£0.00		
	Dec					284					£0.00	£0.00	£0.00		
5	Jan					284					£0.00	£0.00	£0.00		
	Feb					284					£0.00	£0.00	£0.00		
	Mar					284					£0.00	£0.00	£0.00		
	Apr					284					£0.00	£0.00	£0.00		

Fig. 7.5 Investment record.

will allow us to calculate the return on the share taking time into account.

» Column 11: The mid-price of the share at the time that investors are examining performance. This will only be shown once as the current price when you are reviewing the share.

» Column 12: This calculates the selling price as mid-price −2.5% to allow for the costs of the selling transaction.

» Column 13: The net selling value is the number of shares held in column 7 at the end of this month multiplied by the selling price per share in column 12.

» Column 14: We need now to calculate the monthly cashflow, which is simply the net of cash flowing in from dividends and sales minus any costs incurred that month. We will need this column as input to the next calculation.

» Column 15: This is the crux of the form. You have to calculate the internal rate of return of the cashflows of every month since the share was first bought. To do this you will need discounted cashflow (DCF) tables if you are working manually. It is much simpler if you use a financial calculator with internal rate of return (IRR) available as a function or, of course, a computer spreadsheet.

In effect this calculation takes into account the time value of money, allowing for the dates when it was paid out or paid in. This is the theoretically soundest measure of return.

» Column 16: It is normal to compare investments by their annual return, so we need to turn the monthly cashflow into an annual equivalent. The formula for this is:

((1 + monthly cashflow) to the power 12) −1

or in our example:

((1 + 2.57%)^12) −1

The usefulness of this single number echoes the usefulness of DCF in comparing spending projects with each other. No matter how long we have held a share, we can compare its performance against any other share in the portfolio.

For the moment we need to add further complications to Figure 7.5 to see what happens if we make further transactions (Fig. 7.6).

In March of Year 4 the company issued new shares under a rights issue. They offered 1 share for every 10 held, and the investor decided

| | | | | | | | Investment record | | | | Feb May | | | | |

| Name of Company | Oil Integrated | | | | | | | | Usual date of interim dividend | Feb May | | | | | |
| Type of share | Ord 25p | | | | | Year ends | December | | Usual date of final dividend | Aug Nov | | | | | |

Year	Date	Number of shares bought	Bonus issue shares	Rights issues shares	Number of shares sold	Balance held	Month cost	Dividends	Proceeds from sales	Mid price per share	Selling price	Net selling value	Monthly c/f	DCF	Annualized
2	Nov	284				284	1346.16				£0.00	£0.00	-£1,346.16		
	Dec					284					£0.00	£0.00	£0.00		
3	Jan					284					£0.00	£0.00	£0.00		
	Feb					284		£11.36			£0.00	£0.00	£11.36		
	Mar					284					£0.00	£0.00	£0.00		
	Apr					284					£0.00	£0.00	£0.00		
	May					284		12.07			£0.00	£0.00	£12.07		
	Jun					284					£0.00	£0.00	£0.00		
	Jul					284					£0.00	£0.00	£0.00		
	Aug					284		12.07			£0.00	£0.00	£12.07		
	Sep					284					£0.00	£0.00	£0.00		
	Oct					284		14.20			£0.00	£0.00	£14.20		
	Nov					284					£0.00	£0.00	£0.00		
	Dec					284					£0.00	£0.00	£0.00		
4	Jan					284		14.20			£0.00	£0.00	£14.20		
	Feb					284					£0.00	£0.00	£0.00		
	Mar	100		28		512	168		2.40		£0.00	£0.00	£165.60		
	Apr					412	750				£0.00	£0.00	-£750.00		
	May					412		14.20			£0.00	£0.00	£14.20		
	Jun					412					£0.00	£0.00	£0.00		
	Jul					412		20.60			£0.00	£0.00	£20.60		
	Aug					412					£0.00	£0.00	£0.00		
	Sep					412					£0.00	£0.00	£0.00		
	Oct					412		22.25			£0.00	£0.00	£22.25		
	Nov					412					£0.00	£0.00	£0.00		
	Dec					412					£0.00	£0.00	£0.00		
5	Jan					412					£0.00	£0.00	£0.00		
	Feb					412		22.25		8.85	£8.65	£3,555.05	£3,577.30	2.46%	33.86%
	Mar					412					£0.00	£0.00	£0.00		
	Apr										£0.00	£0.00	£0.00		

Fig. 7.6 Investment record.

to take up the offer. The share had done well and they saw no reason why it should not continue to do so. They thus purchased 28 new shares shown in column 5. The price £6 was at a fair discount to the mid-price of the previous month. The expenditure of £168 is in column 8. The balance of shares held, column 7, has increased to 312. The remaining .4 of a share they were owed, since they owned 284, was paid in cash, 40% of £6, which equals £2.40 and is shown as proceeds from sales in column 10.

The following month the investor had some more money to invest and decided to stick with a share that had done very well for him. He invested a further £730 which was the total cost of buying 100 shares at the current buying price of £7.12 plus costs of £18.

The next two quarters of dividends per share were more or less as before, but the payment in November of Year 4 was higher, reflecting a small increase in the dividend. This was repeated in Feb of Year 5 when the share price had risen to £8.85 as quoted in the paper.

On an annualized basis the discounted return on investment of this share now stands at 33.86%.

To make comparisons between shares, investors can now look at their whole portfolio in this way, and make a relevant and consistent comparison among all the shares they hold. This is shown in Figure 7.7.

KEY INSIGHTS

We have seen the enormous value of using the discounted cashflow technique in various ways. If a manager has only internalized one financial technique, probably the most beneficial is the DCF. Accountants get down to some very detailed numbers to produce viable cashflows. But the key insight has to be that the financial techniques are only there as an aid to decision-making. It simplifies the financial part of the decision and enables managers to look at various scenarios before making the best decision in terms of risk and return.

Company	Annualized return	Last date bought	Reference
Oil integrated	36%	Nov-Year 2	S1
Banks, retail	23%	Jan - Year 1	S1
Paper, packaging, printing	23%	Apr-Year 2	S1
Insurance	21%	Feb-Year 1	S1
Health care	19%	Nov-Year 1	S1
Media	18%	May-Year 1	S1
Engineering vehicles	18%	Jul-Year 2	S1
Spirits, wine and ciders	17%	Aug-Year 1	S1
Building and construction	14%	Jan-Year 2	S1
Spirits, wines and ciders	12%	Aug-Year 1	S10
Transport	11%	Jan-Year 3	S11
Telecommunications	11%	Jul-Year 2	S12
Food producers	11%	Jan-Year 1	S13
Retailers general	10%	Jun-Year 1	S14
Pharmaceuticals	10%	Jan-Year 2	S15
American Inv Trust	10%	Apr-Year 1	S16
Gas distribution	6%	May-Year 2	S17
Chinese Inv Trust	5%	Nov-Year 1	S18
Engineering	3%	Oct-Year 2	S19
European Inv Trust	-3%	Jan-Year 3	S20
Emerging Inv Trust	-4%	Jan-Year 3	S21
Chemicals	-5%	Jul-Year 2	S22
Chemicals	-6%	Jan-Year 3	S23
Food producers	-8%	Jan-Year 3	S24
Gas distribution	-10%	Jan-Year 3	S25
Electronic & electrical	-15%	Jul-Year 2	S26
Distributors	-16%	Jan-Year 1	S27
Electronic & electrical	-27%	Oct-Year 2	S28
Average	6.45%		
Transport	11%	Jan-Year 3	
American Inv Trust	-3%	Jan-Year 3	
Emerging Inv Trust	-4%	Jan-Year 3	
Chemicals	-6%	Jan-Year 3	
Food producers	-8%	Jan-Year 3	
Gas distribution	-10%	Jan-Year 3	
Average without shares less than 3 months old	12%		

Fig. 7.7 Portfolio analysis.

Key Concepts and Thinkers

The main part of this chapter describes the key words and concepts used by the finance department.

» Words of wisdom on return on investment from a manager and an investment guru
» Glossary of terms

"A wise man should have money in his head, but not in his heart."
Jonathan Swift, 1667-1745, English churchman and writer

Between this chapter and Chapter 9, I am giving references to people who have written about or who offer particular services in the return on investment arena. But the bulk of this chapter has to be the glossary of financial terms. Have you ever debated an issue with a finance director? They talk in tongues, and if managers and investors are to get the assistance finance people can offer, then they need to be able to talk that language.

But first, two people have had a lot of influence on thinking about return on investment. The first has been concerned with investment appraisal from a customer and supplier's point of view, the second has made people review their thoughts on share portfolio management. The first is Mack Hanan, who took solution selling and complex sales planning to its logical conclusion with his book *Consultative Selling*.[1]

CONSULTATIVE SELLING

Many salespeople assure their prospects and customers that if they buy from them they will be investing in not just a supplier of goods and services, but also a partner for their operation. Many assure, but few actually deliver on this promise. Indeed, if you probe them, few can actually define what a partnership between a customer and a supplier is.

Mack Hanan's book *Consultative Selling* gives as good a definition of the processes involved in becoming your customer's partner as you can get. His starting point is this:

"Consultative selling is profit improvement selling. It is selling to high-level customer decision makers who are concerned with profit – indeed who are responsible for it, measured by it, evaluated by it and accountable for it."

The process involves analyzing trends in the customer's product/markets, researching the customer's business, developing customer strategies for growth, and finally recommending actions that the customer should take to improve their profits. If you do this, Hanan maintains, you will be pretty much immune from competitors because you are offering a much more valuable kind of service. In fact the supplier is more or less going through the same process as the customer.

The consultative selling process includes becoming involved in the customer's evaluation of your proposition from a return on investment perspective.

Hanan says, "An opportunity window opens for [the salesperson] when the following conditions are met:

1 The dollar value of the profits from your solution exceed the dollar value of the customer's problem.
2 The dollar value of the profits from your solution exceed the dollar value of the costs of your solution.
3 The dollar value of the profits from your solution exceed the dollar value of the profits from competitive solutions."

In order to know this, the salesperson has to be privy to the customer's process of investment appraisal, with an emphasis on the financial side, and to be able to assist the customer to estimate the benefits of the solution. It is not easy to get into that position with a customer; it requires a high level of contact and an even higher level of confidence in the salesperson and their integrity. But it can be done as long as the salesperson can ask the right questions and use their, or their own finance people's, knowledge to assist the customer in this way.

As long as the average salesperson still imagines that his or her greatest skill is to describe the features of their products and services in sometimes insufferable detail, professional salespeople who join in the debate about the way ahead for their customers with the senior managers they deal with have an immense competitive edge.

WARREN BUFFET

Kevin Keasey, Robert Hudson and Kevin Littler sum Buffet's philosophy up very well in their book, *The Intelligent Guide to Stock Market Investment.*[2]

They note, first of all, the simple but important attitude to investing that Buffet, still believed by many people to be the greatest investor of all time, advocates. He believes that a successful investor wants to make money and has a great interest in the investment process. They are not, however, greedy and are willing to put in the thinking time it takes to understand a company.

He extols patience regarding the ups and downs of the market as immaterial if you have bought a good company. He is scathing of public opinion, exhorting us to form our own judgment and then stick to it no matter how unpopular it appears to be.

He uses the term "comfortable" in the phrase that Keasey reports, "You should only invest what you feel comfortable with," on the grounds that if you invest more than that, you will not have the patience to see it through. He also advises that investors recognize their own limitations, so as not to go past the depth of their own understanding. And finally, he says that investors should be focused.

Once you have got your attitude right, Buffet gives a checklist of attributes you should look for in a business. Some are very specific, such as looking for businesses that take royalties. Some steer you away from some extremely popular stocks; his most famous advice is that we should not invest in cyclicals or high tech companies. Nor should we look at businesses whose strategies lead them into diversification. His view on those being "One buys two of everything and in the end owns a zoo."

The detail of the checklist is in Keasey's excellent book.

GLOSSARY OF FINANCIAL TERMS

Accounting policies - Those principles and practices applied by an entity that specify how the effects of transactions and other events are to be reflected in the accounts. For example, an entity may have a policy of revaluing fixed assets or of maintaining them at historical cost. Accounting policies do not include estimation techniques.

Accounts payable - American terminology for creditors.

Accounts receivable - American terminology for debtors.

Accrual - An expense or a proportion thereof not invoiced prior to the balance sheet date but included in the accounts sometimes on an estimated basis.

Accruals concept - Income and expenses are recognized in the period in which they are earned or incurred, rather than the period in which they happen to be received or paid.

Asset – Any property or rights owned by the company that have a monetary value. In UK accounting standards, assets are defined as "rights or other access to future economic benefits controlled by an entity as a result of past transactions or events."

Balance sheet – A statement describing what a business owns and owes at a particular date.

Break-even point – The level of activity at which the fixed costs of a project are just covered by the contribution from sales. At this point there is neither a profit nor a loss.

Break-even analysis – A form of analysis that relates activity to totals of revenue and costs based on the classification of costs into fixed and variable.

Capital employed – The aggregate amount of long-term funds invested in or lent to the business and used by it in carrying out its operations.

Cashflow forecast – A statement of future, anticipated cash balances based on estimated cash inflows and outflows over a given period.

Cashflow statement – A statement of cashflows during the most recent accounting period. The required format for a cashflow statement is laid down in accounting standards.

Comparability – The requirement that once an accounting policy for a particular item in the accounts has been adopted the same policy should be used from one period to the next. Any change in policy must be fully disclosed. Comparability is also important when comparing entities in the same industry. They should, wherever possible, use similar accounting policies.

Contingent liability – A possible obligation arising from past events whose existence will be confirmed only by the occurrence of one or more uncertain future events not wholly within the entity's control.

Costs of capital – The weighted average costs of funds to a company based on the mix of equity and loan capital and their respective costs. This is sometimes used as the required rate of return in a discounted cashflow.

Costs of good sold (or Cost of sales) – Those costs (usually raw materials, labor and production overheads) directly attributable to goods that have been sold. The difference between sales and cost of goods sold is gross profit.

Creditors - Amounts due to those who have supplied goods or services to the business.

Current asset - An asset which, if not already in cash form, is expected to be converted into cash within 12 months of the balance sheet date.

Current cost - The convention by which assets are valued at the cost of replacement at the balance sheet date (net of depreciation for fixed assets).

Current liability - An amount owed which will have to be paid within 12 months of the balance sheet date.

Current ratio - The ratio of current assets to current liabilities in a balance sheet, providing a measure of business liquidity.

Debentures - Long-term loans, usually secured on the company's assets.

Debtors - Amounts due from customers to whom goods or services have been sold but for which they have not yet paid.

Deferred asset/liability - An amount receivable or payable more than 12 months after the balance sheet date.

Deferred taxation - An estimate of a tax liability payable at some estimated future date, resulting from timing differences in the taxation and accounting treatment of certain items of income and expenditure.

Depreciation - An estimate of the proportion of the cost of a fixed asset which has been consumed (whether through use, obsolescence, or the passage of time) during the accounting period.

Discounted cashflow (DCF) - A method of appraisal for investment projects. The total incremental stream of cash for a project is tested to assess the level of return it delivers to the investor. If the return exceeds the required, or hurdle, rate the project is recommended on financial terms or vice versa.

Distribution - The amount distributed to shareholders out of the profits of the company, usually in the form of a cash dividend.

Dividend cover - The ratio of the amount of profit reported for the year to the amount distributed.

Dividend yield - The ratio of the amount of dividend per share to the market share price of a listed company.

Earnings per share – The amount of profit (after tax and any extraordinary items) attributable to shareholders divided by the number of ordinary shares in issue.

EBIT – Earnings (profit) before interest and tax.

EBITDA – Earnings (profit) before interest, tax, depreciation, and amortization. This measure of operating cash flow is considered to be an important measure of the performance of an entity.

Estimation techniques – The methods adopted by an entity to arrive at estimated monetary amounts for items in the accounts. For example, of the various methods that could be adopted for depreciation, the entity may select to depreciate using the straight-line method.

Exceptional item – Income or expenditure that, although arising from the ordinary course of business, is of such unusual size or incidence that it needs to be disclosed separately.

Expense – A cost incurred, or a proportion of a cost, the benefit of which is wholly used up in the earning of the revenue for a particular accounting period.

Extraordinary item – Material income or expenditure arising from outside the ordinary course of business. As a result of recent changes to accounting standards, it is considered that extraordinary items are extremely rare if not non-existent.

Fixed asset – Asset held for use by the business rather than for sale.

Fixed cost – A cost that does not vary in proportion to changes in the scale of operations, e.g. rent.

Gearing – Gearing is the word used to describe the financing of the company in terms of the proportion of capital provided by shareholders (equity) compared with the proportion provided by loan capital (debt).

Gearing ratios – There are many different ways to measure gearing. The commonest is probably the ratio of debt to equity. That is the ratio of long-term loans to shareholders' funds (which can be measured in terms of nominal value or market value). Another common approach (called the capital gearing ratio) is to calculate the percentage of debt to total capital (debt plus equity). The income gearing ratio is the ratio of interest payable to the profits out of which interest is paid.

Gross profit – The difference between sales and the cost of goods sold.

Historic cost convention – The convention by which assets are valued on the basis of the original cost of acquiring or producing them.

Hurdle rate – The rate of return decided on by a company as the minimum acceptable for capital investment. It will be governed by the company's cost of capital and it may allow for different levels of risk.

Interest cover – The relationship between the amount of profit (before interest and before tax) and the amount of interest payable during a period.

Internal rate of return (IRR) – The rate of discount that brings the present value of all the cashflows associated with a capital investment to zero. It measures the effective yield on the investment. If this yield is greater than the hurdle rate the investment is seen to be financially desirable and vice versa.

Liability – An amount owed. In UK accounting standards, liabilities are defined as "an entity's obligations to transfer economic benefits as a result of past transactions or events."

Liquidity – A term used to describe the cash resources of a business and its ability to meet its short-term obligations.

Listed investments – Investments the market price for which is quoted on a recognized Stock Exchange. They may therefore be traded on that Exchange.

Long-term liability – An amount payable more than 12 months after the balance sheet date.

Market price – The price of a quoted security for dealing in the open market.

Net assets – The amount of total assets less total liabilities.

Net book value – The cost (or valuation) of fixed assets less accumulated depreciation to date. Net book value bears no relationship to market value.

Net current assets – The amount of current assets less current liabilities.

Net present value (NPV) - A positive or negative value arrived at by discounting the cashflow from a capital project by the desired rate of return. If the value is positive, it means that the project is desirable and vice versa.

Net realizable value - Amount at which an asset could be sold in its existing condition at the balance sheet date, after deducting any costs to be incurred in disposing of it.

Nominal value - The face value of a share or other security.

Opportunity cost - The alternative advantage foregone as a result of the commitment of resources to one particular end.

Overhead - Any expense, other than the direct cost of materials or labor involved in making a company's products.

Payback period - A term used in investment appraisal. It refers to the time required for the non-discounted cash inflow to accumulate to the initial cash outflow in the investment.

Prepayment - The part of a cost which is carried forward as an asset in the balance sheet to be recognized as an expense in the ensuing period(s) in which the benefit will be derived from it, e.g. the payment in advance of rates.

Price/earnings ratio - The relationship between the market price of a share and its latest reported earnings per share.

Profit - The difference between the revenues earned in the period and the costs incurred in earning them. Alternative definitions are possible according to whether the figure is struck before or after tax.

Profit and loss account - A statement summarizing the revenues and the costs incurred in earning them during an accounting period.

Provision - A liability of uncertain timing or amount. A provision should only be recognized in the balance sheet when an entity has a present obligation (legal or constructive) as a result of a past event, it is probable that a transfer of economic benefits will be required to settle the obligation, and a reliable estimate can be made of the amount of the obligation. Unless these conditions are met, no provision should be recognized.

Quick ratio - The ratio of those current assets readily convertible into cash (usually current assets less stock) to current liabilities.

Residual value – A notional cash inflow attributed to a capital project to allow for value remaining in the project at the final year of the assessment.

Revaluation reserve – The increase in value of a fixed asset as a result of a revaluation. This needs to be included in the balance sheet as part of shareholders' funds in order to make the balance sheet balance.

Revenue reserves – The accumulated amount of profit less losses, generated by the company since its incorporation and retained in it. It is usually called "Profit and loss account" in the balance sheet.

Revenue – Money received from selling the product of the business.

Sensitivity analysis – Analysis of the change in the output values of an equation by small changes to the input values. It is used to assess the risk in an investment project.

Share capital – Stated in the balance sheet at its nominal value and (if fully paid, and not subject to any share premium) representing the amount of money introduced into the company by its shareholders at the time the shares were issued.

Shareholders' funds – A measure of the shareholders' total interest in the company, represented by the total of share capital plus reserves.

Share premium – The surplus over and above nominal value received in consideration for the issue of shares.

Turnover – Revenue from sales.

Variable cost – A cost that increases or decreases in line with changes in the level of activity.

Working capital – Current assets less current liabilities, representing the amount a business needs to invest and which is continually circulating in order to finance its stock, debtors and work-in-progress.

Work-in-progress – Goods (or services) in the course of production (or provision) at the balance sheet date.

NOTES

1 Hanan, M. (1995) *Consultative Selling*. AMACOM, New York.
2 Keasey, K., Hudson, R. & Littler, K. (1998) *The Intelligent Guide to Stock Market Investment*. John Wiley & Sons, Chichester.

Resources

References to sources of material to improve the return on investment of a private investor.

» Websites
» Books and articles

"An ex-actress in New York fitted up her Park Avenue apartment as an office and surrounded herself with charts, graphs and financial reports, playing the market by telephone on an increasing scale and with increasing abandon."

Written in 1929 by Frederick Lewis Allen, 1894–1956,
American humorist

If you imagine the charts and graphs on a computer screen rather than a wall of the apartment, then one could be forgiven for thinking that Frederick Allen could make the same remark now about day traders on the Internet. Sure, there have been successes and some have made a fortune, but it is generally felt that day traders on the whole do not make money.

There is, however, as much advice on how to make money from the stock exchange as anyone could possibly get through in a lifetime. The advice comes from a spectrum of sources with a spectrum of motivations. Some are non-profit-making institutions with a mission to increase the number of private investors, others produce hefty documents of company analysis to guide the investor towards shares that make sense for their investment objectives, and finally there are the snake oil dealers offering instant and large fortunes by simply, would you believe, sending them a few dollars for the winning formula. I will deal with four of them in that order.

NATIONAL ASSOCIATION OF INVESTORS CORPORATION

The NAIC was established in the USA in 1951 by four investment clubs. It is a non-profit, tax-exempt organization whose membership consists of investment clubs and individual investors. Its mission is "to provide a program of sound investment information, education and support that helps create successful, lifetime investors. NAIC's programs, services, and products are designed to help individuals of all knowledge levels to become successful, long-term investors. NAIC members' investment portfolios have consistently outperformed market averages. NAIC has provided investment education to more than five million individuals and is a charter member of the World Federation of Investors, providing investment education in over 17 countries worldwide."

Investment philosophy

NAIC encourages its members to follow four principles when investing.

» Invest a set amount regularly, usually once a month, regardless of market conditions.
» Reinvest all dividends and capital gains.
» Buy growth stocks – companies whose sales are increasing at a rate faster than industry in general.
» Diversify your portfolio – invest in different industries and different size companies.

Membership

As of November 2000, NAIC's membership is comprised of the following:

» NAIC's membership – 537,150 individual and investment club members;
» investment clubs – 35,810 clubs;
» individuals – 47,187 members; and
» computer group – 9,595 members.

From the NAIC Website you can get to everything you need to become an investor from the beginner to the seasoned campaigner:

» www.better-investing.org

PROSHARE

ProShare is a British, independent, not-for-profit organization limited by guarantee and founded in 1992. It was founded by HM Treasury, the London Stock Exchange, and a consortium of major companies to "Promote responsible share based investment, including employee share ownership, primarily through education and research."

ProShare (UK) Ltd is currently funded through charitable donations from over 180 companies and by grants from the London Stock Exchange, The Gatsby Charitable Trust, and The John Templeton Foundation.

Perhaps their biggest emphasis now, and one with which I can easily identify, is on investment clubs. Proshare sell a manual that covers all you need to get a club started and administer it. The club is simply a group of individuals who agree to put in a certain amount of investment money on a monthly basis, and invest it on the stock exchange, choosing shares suggested and researched by members. Club members have very different objectives, from using the club as a learning method before setting up their own portfolio to being like a unit trust as a long-term savings vehicle.

The one I have been in for eight years has a simple objective: to outperform the average unit trust in the UK by investing in UK companies and overseas companies through investment trusts. We have comfortably met this objective; not, I fear, because of our brilliance in picking shares, but because we do not have any costs. There is no-one taking 1.5% of the fund at the beginning of each year, or charging 6% of the investment money as it goes into the fund.

» www.proshare.org

COMPANY REFS

Company refs is a major reference book containing information about UK companies. According to its Website:

"It gives you all the information you need to make an investment decision on a company – saving you hours of research time."

» Where do you turn to when you hear of a company you'd like to know more about?
» How do you get an objective analysis of the shares in your portfolio?
» Where can you find out which shares top the league tables for your favorite indicators – whether it's growth forecast, dividend yield or ROCE?
» Which directors have been buying or selling their company's shares over the last six months?

The answer to all these questions and many more can be found in REFS."

It certainly is very comprehensive, and may very well be a method by which you can achieve success on the stock exchange.

A major contributor to *Company refs* is Jim Slater who helped HS Financial Publishing (formerly Hemmington Scott Ltd) devise and develop *Company refs*.

Jim Slater is also the author of *Beyond the Zulu Principle*, an extension of his stock picking system, the Zulu Principle. Like all methodologies the Zulu Principle has in the past produced results. It has, also, in common with every other type of stock picking method, got it wrong for periods of time. I suspect that is the clue for anyone looking for a method of choosing winning shares; they have worked in the past and they will probably work again in the future – the problem is to pick the time right.

» www.companyrefs.com

THE PINPOINT TRADING METHOD

According to Robert Gudino, you can: "Turn the Stock Market into you (*sic*) personal ATM cash machine."

The PinPoint trading method is, according to Mr Gudino, 80% to 90% accurate. He is only going to train 50 students in his step by step method to pinpoint market tops and bottoms, and, would you believe, he thinks that the less you know about trading, the more successful you will be using his method.

If we had used the method in June 2001, we could have made $2,000 in three days trading on the NASDAQ. He claims that using the method we will make $300 to $1,000 a day. He will change our lives. He has been his own boss for three years.

You must expect to have to pay a lot of money for this limited edition offer; perhaps 25% of your winnings would still be well worth it. But no, the method is yours for $97. It's a snip, and once I have fulfilled this contract with my publisher, I am going to send the $97 and leave this humdrum workaday life of business writing to be a day trader. Or shall I just stick the royalties on 36 red?

» www.robertgudino.com

BOOKS

Katz, J. & McCormick, D. (2000) *Encyclopedia of Trading Strategies*. Irwin, Chicago.

Andrew Burke, A. (1999) *Market Speculating*. Rowton Press.

Graham, B. (1997) *The Intelligent Investor*, 4th edn. HarperCollins (Investment), London.

Keasey, K., Hudson, R. & Littler, K. (1998) *The Intelligent Guide to Stock Market Investment*. John Wiley & Sons, Chichester.

The Wall Street Journal and the *Financial Times* both run personal finance pages on a Saturday. Despite coming from the financial heavies, both aim to help beginners as well as experienced investors to make the most of their money.

Merz, K.J. & Rosen, J. (1997) *The Handbook of Investment Technology*. Irwin, Chicago.

Walsh, C. (1994) *Key Management Ratios*. Pitman Publishing, London.

Covello, J.A. & and Hazelgren, B.F. (1994) *The Complete Book of Business Plans*. Small Business Sourcebooks, Naperville, Ill.

Ten Steps to Evaluating Return on Investment

Financial theory is one thing; putting it into practice another. Chapter 10 provides some key insights into using a useful model to compare one project with another and with a benchmark

- » Document your strategy
- » Communicate your strategy
- » Use the business template
- » List your opportunities
- » Estimate the costs
- » Estimate the benefits
- » Weight the project for risk
- » Use the return on investment model
- » Make the decision
- » Consider the electronic version of the model

"Response to AOL founders seeking venture capital in 1985: 'It's a dog. You should take it out back and shoot it.''

Unknown banker

So now we need to pull it together in a ten-step strategy for looking at an investment opportunity and comparing it with any other using a reliable, relevant, and consistent model.

In trying to keep this chapter as practical as possible, I have to make two assumptions. The first is that a person following this guide is either at board level or leading a team further down the organization. We will see how the cascading of strategy, for example, should put actual candidates for evaluation well into the context of the business – the holistic approach.

Second, no matter where your team sits in your organization, I have to assume that you can, and probably have, defined who your customers are and how they can be grouped together to form markets. Whether they are internal or external to your organization, you have customers, and their importance in deciding on your future investment strategy will be taken into account.

The main steps have been introduced in Chapter 3 and Chapter 6. So what follows are mainly tips from experience, and, of course, at step eight the return on investment model itself.

1. DOCUMENT YOUR STRATEGY

No matter where you are in the organization you need to be able to fill in this form. Group your products services and markets, and put down your targets in terms of sales revenues, profits, resources working in each cell, and any other information that is relevant for your particular team.

Make sure you get people to think creatively at this point. A lot of teams fossilize and get reorganized, or die, because they do not recognize new opportunities or threats to their current product/markets (see Table 10.1).

2. COMMUNICATE YOUR STRATEGY

Now make absolutely certain that everyone who needs to know what the strategy is, does know. Look at how you present this to different

Table 10.1 Strategy form.

Activity matrix	Market 1	Market 2	Market 3	Market 4	Market 5	Market 6	Market 7	Market 8
Product 1								
Product 2								
Product 3								
Product 4								
Product 5								

types of person. I have seen a large electricity company putting up copies of its mission statement for all to see. It did not mean a lot to a storekeeper running the spares warehouse in a remote country setting. Think about what you need to tell each person and how you should tell them.

Here are some thought starters for how you might represent the strategy to different groups. The detailed report of the whole plan will suit people who are heavily engaged in its implementation. Perhaps you should confine this to your manager and some key team members. If everyone sends out their strategy to everyone else, everyone will drown in plans.

You need an outline report with a summary, personalized to each stakeholder you send it to, concentrating on the parts that have a direct impact on them. Remember the objective of this – you want them to be able to evaluate current and future projects and activities against this plan.

A regular, but not too frequent, presentation of the report is often advisable to your peer group. They are probably the most likely team leaders to come up with suggestions for improvement. Then you have the normal PR job with newsletters and so on giving updates on the strategy.

3. USE THE BUSINESS-CASE TEMPLATE

Look at your strategy and the one that you are operating under, and use the business-case template from Chapter 6. As the linkage between all strategies from the Board down, the business-case template is a very important tool. It keeps current activities focused, or changes them, and encourages everyone to search for new ways of doing things and new things to do.

4. LIST YOUR OPPORTUNITIES

A lot of teams define fewer activities as being part of a project than they should. A project is a series of activities designed to achieve a specific outcome within a set budget to a specified timescale. I have often found it helpful when acting as a consultant to encourage teams to look at what they do and make sure they have identified all the activities that should be part of a project, and all the activities that should be part of a process. Once you have identified all your projects and processes and checked them against the business-case template, you are in a position to move confidently to the tactical part of calculating return on investment knowing that what you are looking at will, if you decide to implement it, assist the strategy rather than oppose it.

5. ESTIMATE THE COSTS

Not much to add here except to say that there is out there a prevalent attitude amongst experienced managers that projects will go over budget and, guess what, statistics prove that they are right. You will obviously get as much as possible of your supplier's products and services at a fixed price – that helps predictability. But that has a down side too. I discovered when I was selling computer solutions that if I exerted enough pressure on the company that was supplying software, by threatening them with our losing to a competing solution, I could get them to cut out most if not all of their contingency budget. This brought down the price but greatly increased the risk that we would not be able to deliver. As usual it is a balance.

6. ESTIMATE THE BENEFITS

If you follow Mack Hanan's advice from *Consultative Selling* (see Chapter 8) and assist clients to build a return on investment case for purchasing what you supply, you will find the process is as much about bargaining as it is about logic. This is true too for the managers inside a business.

I was once selling a computer solution to a production line problem in a glass-making factory. The solution automated part of the bottle production process. Its benefits were in productivity terms. Put simply, manpower currently on the production lines could be moved elsewhere or lost. The question was "How many?"

During the early part of the selling cycle I got agreement from the production director that 32 people could be saved in this way. When I spoke to his direct reports, who supervised the production lines, they were cynical about this prediction, saying that whilst they agreed that they had too many people, they did not believe that more than 16 could be removed without affecting quality. I wrote the number 16 into the selling proposal, attributing my source as the production director. When he saw the draft of my proposal he came back swiftly and said I could not use that figure in a report going to his boss, because his headcount would be cut by that number no matter how efficiently or otherwise the new system worked. During a phone call he agreed to my quoting just 8 people savings. It still worked out, and I had learnt a lot about the practical reality of making a business case.

7. WEIGHT THE PROJECT FOR RISK

We have looked at the issue of risk in a generic sense (see Chapter 6), and it is covered generically in the model that follows at step eight. To summarize – complex projects can easily go wrong. They are difficult to predict and plan, and things will change during the lifetime of such a project. That is why two things follow good risk assessment. The first is that you modify the financial predictions to allow for risk, and the second that you build a contingency plan for the times when a predicted risk does occur. Of course you will not be able to predict everything, but have a plan for the worst that you can foresee.

If no contingency is available for a project and the risks are high impact and high probability, then that should weigh heavily on a go/no go decision on the project.

8. USE THE RETURN ON INVESTMENT MODEL

Purpose (why)

To get a financial indicator of the return on investment of a project, in order to compare one project to any other.

Principles

» Using this model gives a consistent measure and makes sure that you are comparing like with like.

» The tool takes into account the relative riskiness of the project for comparison purposes.

» The tool points out where extra effort may be required to make sure that the financial objectives of the project are achieved.

» The tool eventually reduces every project to a single comparable number.

Application (how)

Figure 10.1 illustrates the model itself.

Enter first the reference material (Table 10.2).

9. MAKE A DECISION

Figure 10.2 illustrates the model filled in for a proposal to start to produce a new product in a food processing company.

Since the NPV dependency was set at the expected case, we can assume that this case passes the hurdle rate of return with its expected case NPV at £281,000 positive. That does not of itself make the decision for managers. They have then to look at the strategic fit of the project using the business-case template and at other ways that they could invest the money. Then they are in a good position to make a decision.

10. CONSIDER THE ELECTRONIC VERSION OF THE MODEL

Available on the Express Exec web site, ExecutiveExpress.com, is the tool that echoes the methodologies in this book. By using it you will be able to fill in the data speedily and, perhaps more importantly, store the analyses for future reference or for the use of other people in your organization if the tool is available to them.

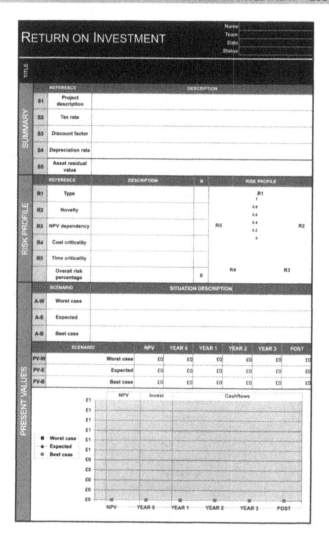

Fig. 10.1 Return on investment model.

		FORECASTS	YEAR 0	YEAR 1	YEAR 2	YEAR 3	POST
WORST CASE	B1	Cost reduction/avoidance					
	B2	Revenue growth					
	B3	Capital expenditure					
	C1	Operating costs					
	C2	Operating cashflow	£0	£0	£0	£0	
	V1	Tax			£0	£0	£0
	V2	Tax - capital allowances			£0	£0	£0
	V3	Residual value				£0	
	V4	Cashflow	£0	£0	£0	£0	£0
	V5	Present value	£0	£0	£0	£0	£0
	V6	Net present value (NPV)	£0				

		FORECASTS	YEAR 0	YEAR 1	YEAR 2	YEAR 3	POST
EXPECTED	B1	Cost reduction/avoidance					
	B2	Revenue growth					
	B3	Capital expenditure					
	C1	Operating costs					
	C2	Operating cashflow	£0	£0	£0	£0	
	V1	Tax			£0	£0	£0
	V2	Tax - capital allowances			£0	£0	£0
	V3	Residual value				£0	
	V4	Cashflow	£0	£0	£0	£0	£0
	V5	Present value	£0	£0	£0	£0	£0
	V6	Net present value (NPV)	£0				

		FORECASTS	YEAR 0	YEAR 1	YEAR 2	YEAR 3	POST
BEST CASE	B1	Cost reduction/avoidance					
	B2	Revenue growth					
	B3	Capital expenditure					
	C1	Operating costs					
	C2	Operating cashflow	£0	£0	£0	£0	
	V1	Tax			£0	£0	£0
	V2	Tax - capital allowances			£0	£0	£0
	V3	Residual value				£0	
	V4	Cashflow	£0	£0	£0	£0	£0
	V5	Present value	£0	£0	£0	£0	£0
	V6	Net present value (NPV)	£0				

Fig. 10.1 (*Continued*).

Table 10.2

Group	No.	Reference	Description	
Summary	S1	Project description	A short description of the project	
	S2	Tax rate	What is the marginal tax rate the tool should use for charging tax for increased profits and claiming allowances for expenditure? If you do not require to take tax into account, set this box to zero	Do not put in the percentage sign, since the model is set to regard this number as a percentage
	S3	Discount factor	What is the rate of return the project is required to exceed? This may be a standard for the organization. As long as a consistent rate is used the RoI tool will make a relevant comparison amongst projects. You may have to revisit this after you have done a risk analysis on the project. Managers generally expect a high-risk project to offer a higher rate of return than a low-risk one. Take account of this when setting this "hurdle" discount factor.	Rule of thumb: If inflation is at 3%, a discount factor of 7% would be a low returning project, 12% a good return and anything over 20% an excellent return. Be careful, though, this rule of thumb is different for different industries.

Table 10.2 (*Continued*).

Group	No.	Reference	Description
	S4	Depreciation rate	Enter the annual depreciation rate. Do not put in the percentage sign, since the model is set to regard this number as a percentage	The tool uses this to calculate the tax cashflow. It allows tax against this depreciation rate in each of the three years of the project.
	S5	Residual value percentage	At the end of three years some expenditure on capital items may have a residual value. What is the percentage residual value at the end of the three-year project analysis? If it will have no value, set this box to zero.	Your organization may have a rule for this. If it will be the amount not written off in depreciation, you will have to work out what this figure should be, e.g. if depreciation is set at 25%, then the unwritten down percentage will be 25%, which is what you should enter here.
Risk profile	R1	Type	What is the predominant type of benefit from this project = cost reduction (least risky), cost avoidance (middle risk) or revenue growth (most risky)?	Each of these risks is set an indicator from 1 to 10, where 1 is very low risk and 10 is extremely high.

When looking at the benefits of an investment, generally speaking there is much less risk in achieving cost reductions and cost avoidance than revenue growth. If the project is mainly concerned with cost reduction you should set the risk indicator, the next column, fairly low. If the benefits are mainly concerned with avoiding costs that would occur if this project were not implemented, mark the risk medium. If all the benefits are concerned with growing revenues, then it is a high-risk project and should be marked as such.

| R2 | Novelty | How novel are the activities involved in carrying out this project:

(a) routine;
(b) modification to existing project;
(c) new type of project.

There is a low risk if the project is a repeat of things the organization has done before. If the organization has operated in a similar way before, then

Table 10.2 (*Continued*).

Group	No.	Reference	Description
	R3	NPV dependency	mark the risk medium. If this project is entirely new, then mark the risk high. At what level of business case must this project give the appropriate NPV? (a) Must pass on worst-case assumptions. (b) Must pass on expected assumptions. (c) Must pass on best-case assumptions. There are three levels of assumptions in the tool if you choose to use them. Worst-case assumptions describe the worst case in terms of the benefits. Expected are your best estimates of what is most likely actually to occur, and best-case assumptions are the best you could hope for. If there are also different levels of risk on costs, then do the two exercises separately. That is, take the expected level of benefits and compare it to the three levels of costs. Otherwise, take the

expected level of costs and compare it against the three levels of benefits.

If the project is required to achieve its return on investment rate on the worst-case level of benefits, mark the project low risk. If it is required to achieve the expected level of benefits, then mark it as medium risk, and if it can go ahead on the best-case benefits, mark it as high risk. You may also combine the estimates. For example, if you combine the worst-case costs and benefits you get the overall worst case.

R4   Cost criticality

How cost critical is the project?
(a) Budgets are not important.
(b) Budgets are normal.
(c) Budgets are very tight.

How critical is it that the project remains within its budget. If there is easy access to more funds, mark it as low risk. If some more money could be made available, mark it as medium.

Table 10.2 (*Continued*).

Group	No.	Reference	Description
			If there is absolutely no further money available, mark it as high risk.
	R5	Time criticality	How time critical is the project? (a) Timing is not important. (b) Timing is of normal importance. (c) Timing is a tight window-of-opportunity. If there is plenty of slippage time available, mark this as low. If it is important that this project is completed on time, then mark it medium. If there is a window of time available that must be achieved, mark this as high risk. If the overall percentage risk is around 50 you have a medium risk project, well above 50 is high, and well below is low. If the risk is extreme in either direction, you may care to review the discount factor that the project must beat.

Assumptions	A-W	Worst case	On what assumptions have you based the worst-case scenario? Describe the possibilities here.
	A-E	Expected case	On what assumptions have you based the expected-case scenario? Describe the possibilities here.
	A-B	Best case	On what assumptions have you based the best-case scenario? Describe the possibilities here.
Present values	PV-W	Worst case	These represent the present value of the cashflows year by year for the worst case. The total value, the single number that you can use for comparison, is called the Net Present Value or NPV.
	PV-E	Expected case	These represent the present value of the cashflows year by year for the expected case. The total value, the single number that you can use for comparison, is called the Net Present Value or NPV.
	PV-B	Best case	These represent the present value of the cashflows year by year for the best case. The total value, the single number that

Table 10.2 (*Continued*).

Group	No.	Reference	Description
			you can use for comparison, is called the Net Present Value or NPV.

The items for B1 to V6 have the same definition for each of the three cases – worst, expected, and best.

Group	No.	Reference	Description
Each of the three cases	B1	Benefits Cost reduction and avoidance	What is the amount of cost that you are expending at the moment that will be saved through the implementation of this project?
			What are the costs that would occur if you do not implement this project, and what costs would be avoided?
	B2	Benefits Revenue growth	What additional revenues will occur as a result of implementing this project?
	C1	Cost	What capital expenditure does the implementation of this project require?
			You may find that there are specific rules in your organization to distinguish capital expenditure on this line from revenue expenditure on C1 in Years 1, 2 and 3.

C2	Cost	What are the continuing running costs of this project?	
C3	Operating cashflow	The tool calculates the year by year cashflow of this project.	
V1	Tax	Using the tax rate you gave at S3, the tool charges tax on the benefits of the project and allows tax against capital and revenue expenditure.	If you have set S3 at 0, then the tool will ignore all tax considerations.
V2	Tax – capital allowances	The tool calculates tax allowances on capital expenditure as the capital value minus the residual value times the depreciation rate times the tax rate.	You may have to check that this is relevant for your organization.
V3	Residual value	The tool calculates the residual value from the percentage you gave at S5 and puts this in as a positive cashflow item at Year 3.	
V4	Cashflow	This is the year by year cashflow of the project	

Table 10.2 (*Continued*).

Group	No	Reference	Description
	V5	Present value	This is the present value of the cashflows discounted by the factor you entered in S4.
	V6	Net present value	This is a cross add of the present values to give the net present value. If this figure is positive, it means that the project does meet the rate of return in S4. If it is negative, it does not meet that rate. The higher this number is, the better the return on investment. This is the single number you can use to compare one project with another financially.

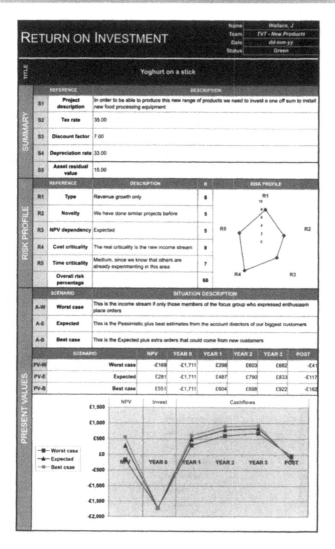

Fig. 10.2 Return on investment model: new product.

WORST CASE

	FORECASTS	YEAR 0	YEAR 1	YEAR 2	YEAR 3	POST
B1	Cost reduction/avoidance					
B2	Revenue growth		£465	£815	£815	
B3	Capital expenditure	£1,711				
C1	Operating costs		£146	£181	£182	
C2	Operating cashflow	-£1,711	£319	£634	£633	
V1	Tax			-£112	-£222	-£221
V2	Tax - capital allowances			£168	£168	£168
V3	Residual value				£257	
V4	Cashflow	-£1,711	£319	£690	£836	-£54
V5	Present value	-£1,711	£298	£603	£682	-£41
V6	Net present value (NPV)	-£169				

EXPECTED

	FORECASTS	YEAR 0	YEAR 1	YEAR 2	YEAR 3	POST
B1	Cost reduction/avoidance					
B2	Revenue growth		£667	£1,099	£1,099	
B3	Capital expenditure	£1,711				
C1	Operating costs		£146	£181	£182	
C2	Operating cashflow	-£1,711	£521	£918	£917	
V1	Tax			-£182	-£321	-£321
V2	Tax - capital allowances			£168	£168	£168
V3	Residual value				£257	
V4	Cashflow	-£1,711	£521	£904	£1,020	-£153
V5	Present value	-£1,711	£487	£790	£833	-£117
V6	Net present value (NPV)	£281				

BEST CASE

	FORECASTS	YEAR 0	YEAR 1	YEAR 2	YEAR 3	POST
B1	Cost reduction/avoidance					
B2	Revenue growth		£792	£1,267	£1,267	
B3	Capital expenditure	£1,711				
C1	Operating costs		£146	£181	£182	
C2	Operating cashflow	-£1,711	£646	£1,086	£1,085	
V1	Tax			-£226	-£380	-£380
V2	Tax - capital allowances			£168	£168	£168
V3	Residual value				£257	
V4	Cashflow	-£1,711	£646	£1,028	£1,130	-£212
V5	Present value	-£1,711	£504	£898	£922	-£162
V6	Net present value (NPV)	£551				

Fig. 10.2 (*Continued*).

KEY LEARNING POINTS

Always check the strategic fit on an investment decision as well as the tactical business case. This also applies to personal investment decisions; only buy shares that fit your investment strategy, and also, borrow only in the context of your financial lifestyle and strategy.

Frequently Asked Questions (FAQs)

Q1: Can I go through a logical process to compare one investment opportunity with another?

A: See Chapter 10.

Q2: How do I make sure that project opportunities have strategic fit?

A: See Chapter 6.

Q3: Can I define and use the technique of discounting cashflows?

A: See Chapter 3.

Q4: Do I know how companies can be valued using return on investment techniques?

A: See Chapter 4.

Q5: Can I distinguish relevant costs and income to put into an investment appraisal model?

A: See Chapter 3.

Q6: Can I access useful investment advice on the Internet?

A: See Chapter 4.

Q7: Do I understand financial terminology well enough to converse with a finance director?

A: See Chapter 8.

Q8: Do I understand how to take cultural differences into account when implementing a return on investment process?

A: See Chapter 5.

Q9: Can I build a cashflow from a profit and loss account?

A: See Chapter 2.

Q10: Do I have access to tools to help keep my return on investment knowledge and skills up to date on a regular basis?

A: See Chapter 10.

Index